WHAT TO BUY FOR YOUR BABY

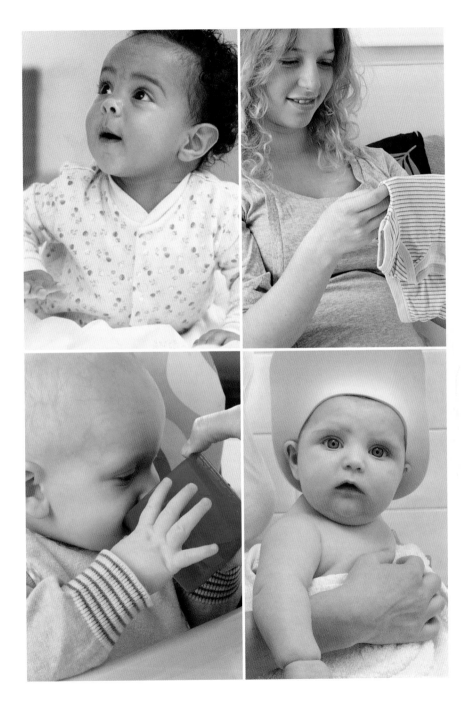

WHAT TO BUY FOR YOUR BABY

ALL YOU NEED TO KNOW TO SPEND YOUR MONEY WISELY

**LIAT HUGHES JOSHI
& CAROLINE COSGROVE**

CARROLL & BROWN LIMITED

To our husbands, Dhaval and Nick, for enduring endless discussions of baby products. To our children, Luca, Juliette and James, for inadvertently getting us started on this whole baby gear thing in the first place. Finally to our own parents; buying for your baby was definitely a lot simpler in your day!

First published in 2012 in the United Kingdom by

Carroll & Brown Limited
20 Lonsdale Road
London NW6 6RD

Text copyright © Liat Hughes Joshi
and Caroline Cosgrove 2012
Compilation copyright
© Carroll & Brown Limited 2012

A CIP catalogue record for this book
is available from the British Library.

ISBN 978-1-907952-28-9
10 9 8 7 6 5 4 3 2 1

Printed in China

Front cover, p6, © I Love Images/Corbis

CONTENTS

THANK GOODNESS FOR THE NINE MONTHS NOTICE

Welcome to the world of baby shopping! Preparing for your new arrival is a truly exciting time, but it can also be confusing. Nursery shops are crammed with products designed to tempt you to part with your cash and the amount of choice out there can be thoroughly overwhelming. What's more you're buying for a person you've never even met!

You're going to encounter items you probably didn't even know existed before conceiving and sometimes you'll wish you had a special 'baby kit' dictionary to decipher the terminology. Take prams: there are two-in-ones, three-in-ones, travel systems, three-wheelers, buggies, umbrella folders, telescopic folders – it's almost enough to bring on early labour. It also can seem that everyone you know is offering conflicting advice. One friend swears by her fancy nappy disposal bin with its deodorising refill cartridges, another thinks it's an insane waste of money. One friend waxes lyrical about baby slings, another just couldn't get the hang of hers.

Advice on internet forums is no more definitive and online reviews can be helpful but aren't always what they seem (be warned that some are 'sponsored' by companies keen to ensure their products get positive recommendations). Head to the shops and who knows whether that assistant has your best interests or their sales figures at heart?

Well, this is where we come in – to help you cut through the confusion so you can make your own, informed decisions about what you want to buy for your baby. Whether you'd like a basic, clear list of essentials or to delve further into the pros and cons of microwave, cold water or steam sterilisers or what to consider when choosing a car seat, we're here to help. Think of us as your own personal shoppers, guiding you impartially through the jungle of baby kit and easing some of the stress of preparing for your newborn's arrival.

Baby gear can be surprisingly controversial and many choices are quite personal; not everyone will agree with everything we say (feel free to email us your views at comments@whattobuyforyourbaby.co.uk or tweet us at @babygearguru) but we've consulted far and wide, and assembled our very own 'parent panel' – a group of knowledgeable parents who've been there, done that and have the bags under their eyes to show for it. We've put their views together with our own extensive experience of baby products – both professional and as mothers – to provide you with all the information you need to make decisions.

We hope that by using this book, 'baby shopping' will be fun and stress-free rather than the chore it can easily become. Perhaps with our help you can spend a little less time waddling around nursery shops and a little more time resting those swollen ankles and supping a nice cup of decaf.

Liat Hughes Joshi
Caroline Cosgrove

MAKING SHOPPING EASIER

At the beginning of each chapter, we've included a list of what's on offer. This is a snapshot view of which items are essential, optional (depending on your circumstances or preferences) or which, in our view, will more than likely gather dust. (At the back of the book, you will find a complete, detachable, shopping list plus baby gift wish lists.)

Then we go on to discuss each item in detail. Where there are choices (and believe us there are many), we discuss the pros and cons of the main options. Although we mention our favourite brands and specific products, this is not our main focus; products change quickly and there are too many to cover here anyway. When we do recommend particular brands, rest assured: we're entirely independent with no vested interests.

Throughout the book you'll also find various tip boxes (see symbols key opposite page) and, at the back, details of useful shopping and information websites.

KEY TO SHOPPING LISTS

✓ Indicates an essential. Occasionally this refers to something that you could in theory manage without but which we thoroughly recommend to make life easier.

? Optional buys. These are useful or helpful items but you can certainly live without them.

✗ Things we think aren't worth spending money on. There will always be someone who disagrees, but on the whole, we think it's best to leave such items on the nursery shop's shelf.

Star buys These are our recommended buys for product categories. A star buy won't necessarily be cheap but it will, in our opinion, offer good value for what it is and be among the best of its type at the time of writing. If none appears, it's because products of that type are fairly similar (see Worth considering) or we don't recommend buying in that category.

Worth considering Good options where no one product stands out sufficiently or the items differ in cost or features from the starred buys so may suit your personal circumstances better.

Safety tip Accompanying this symbol, you will find information and advice to help you keep your baby safe.

 Parent panel tip Under this symbol, you will find products or ways of doing things that our parent panel has found helpful or useful.

 Twin tip The two baby faces signal advice for those expecting twins or more.

 Top tip A yellow daisy should alert you to valuable information that we want to share but that can't be categorised under another heading!

Eco-friendly Under this symbol we include advice on 'green' products and/or being environmentally friendly. A ✿ in the star buys or worth considering lists indicates an organic item.

Money saving tips and pricing guide The shopping cart heads up at-a-glance pricing information and/or money-saving tips. These include recommendations for multi-functional items you'll get lots of use out of, cheap and cheerful products that do the job just as well as pricier alternatives, and good old-fashioned advice that can help you cut down on spending. **£–£££+** indicates cost of items relative to each other: **£** being the cheapest and **£££+** the most expensive.

◗ *Looking ahead*
After this symbol, we mention items that may be needed once your baby is older.

PRODUCT SHOWCASE

These are items, which stand out from the crowd; they might be unusual, new innovations or especially good value for what they are.

SOME PRACTICALITIES

WHEN TO START

We often get asked when is the best time to begin shopping for baby things; we recommend starting some time after the 20-week scan. By then you'll probably be mentally ready to prepare for your baby's arrival but you'll still have plenty of time for deliberation. Don't leave it all too late as some items have long lead times, or might be out of stock. And, of course, babies can arrive early!

Some religions and cultures prefer parents-to-be to delay purchases until after the birth; if this applies to you, do as much window shopping and planning as possible and then get a friend or relative to collect everything while you're in hospital. Or use the 'delayed delivery' services offered by some retailers, where you select items in advance but only pay and receive them after the birth.

IF YOU DON'T KNOW THE BABY'S SEX

If you prefer not to know ahead of the birth whether you're having a boy or a girl, consider these options when shopping:

❋ Buy everything but choose clothing, equipment and other items in neutral colourways (green, yellow and white, for example) and patterns (stripes, plaids and geometrics) that work for both genders.
❋ Buy neutral essentials and then wait until after the birth for everything else.
❋ Buy both boyish and girly things from shops with good returns and exchange policies.

Particularly if you intend to have more children, it's wise to go with gender-neutral choices for major items anyway. While a pink pram or ballerina-embellished furniture might be lovely for a girl, what if she's joined by a younger brother one day and you want to reuse these products?

HELP I'M HAVING MORE THAN ONE!

If you're expecting twins or more, baby shopping brings a few extra challenges and certainly extra costs. On the whole, the decisions you need to make will be similar to those for just one baby but where there are special considerations, we've included 'twin tips'. For further advice on preparing for twins check out the Twins and Multiple Births Association's website – www.tamba.org.uk.

HOW MUCH IS THIS GOING TO COST?

There's no simple answer. It depends on your financial situation, whether you're a designer-label fan or a thrifty type (by choice or necessity) and how much you can and want to borrow or buy secondhand.

According to an SMA Nutrition survey, the average parents-to-be spent a daunting £1,369 on baby stuff before the birth. One in seven spent between £2,000 and £2,500 and a few coughed up a staggering £5,800 plus.

There truly is no need to spend so much. e-Bay, NCT 'nearly new' sales and friends with older children are all excellent sources of secondhand kit. In the relevant chapters, we cover which items are well suited to secondhand purchase or borrowing from friends or family, and what to look out for when doing so, as safety standards may have changed since the items were originally purchased.

Whether you're after a bargain, some luxuries or just practical advice, we're here to help – happy shopping!

PRE-BIRTH ESSENTIALS

This is the stuff we recommend that you have ready before the birth. Other items listed as essential in the book won't be needed the day you get home from hospital (although you might choose to have them ready before the birth anyway). For more information and quantities see the relevant chapters.

* *Clothing basics* Newborn bodysuits, sleepsuits, scratch mitts, socks, hats, cardigans, bibs.
* *Nappies* plus storage for used nappies if using washables.
* *Nappy sacks*.
* *Changing bag or equivalent* This could be any large-ish bag you already own.
* *Appropriate sleeping place* Moses basket/carrycot/crib/hammock or cot.
* *Bedding* for the above (mattress protector, sheets and blankets).
* *Cottonwool*.
* *A soft towel* solely for your baby's use.
* *Muslin squares*.
* *Nipple cream and breast pads*.
* *Baby bottles, formula and steriliser* if you intend to bottlefeed from birth.
* *Group 0+ car seat*.

LESS OBVIOUS LIFESAVERS

None of these are baby products per se but they can all be a blessing in disguise during those hectic postnatal weeks.

- ❋ *Takeaway menus* for when you can't face cooking.
- ❋ *Supermarket online shopping services* for when you can't face shopping.
- ❋ *Smart phone* for when you're pinned down by a feeding/ sleeping baby.
- ❋ *Post-it notes* for when you're too tired to remember anything.
- ❋ *Microwave* so that you occasionally get a hot meal.
- ❋ *Earplugs and eyemask* for extra zzz's during those daytime 'sleep when your baby sleeps' naps.
- ❋ *Dimmer light switch* so that night feeds disturb you less.
- ❋ *Stain remover* for when nappies leak!
- ❋ *A variety of batteries* for your baby's electronic equipment or toys.

CHAPTER 1

CLOTHING AND SHOES

SHOPPING FOR CLOTHES

Browsing through rails of utterly adorable little baby clothes can melt the heart of even the least clucky parent-to-be. Cravings for these tiny outfits can be as strong as any for gherkins or pineapple pizza. But it's all too easy to end up with a wardrobe full of barely used baby clothes, so before you head to that shop till, arms (or basket, or even trolley) piled high, consider a couple of things.

SHOPPING LIST

- ✓ Sleepsuits *(6 in newborn size; 6 in the next size up)*
- ✓ Short-sleeved bodysuits *(6–8 in newborn size; 6–8 in the next size up)*
- ✓ 2 cardigans in 0–3 months size *(lightweight for summer, medium-weight for winter)*
- ✓ 4 pairs of socks
- ✓ 2 hats
- ✓ 2 pairs of mittens *(winter babies only)*
- ✓ 2 pairs of scratch mitts
- ✓ 2–3 bibs
- ? 2–3 sleepgowns

First up, you'll almost certainly get stacks of clothes as presents. When we had our babies we were surprised and touched by people's generosity. OK, a few of the gifts were truly hideous (the hand-knitted, misshapen, lurid orange dungarees), some utterly inappropriate for the season (a newborn-size snowsuit for a July baby) but many of the gifts were lovely.

Secondly, new babies grow very quickly and that tremendously tempting designer outfit might literally get just one or two wears before it's stretching at the seams. If you calculate the cost-per-wear, well, it gets scary.

Of course we know how hard it is to resist purchasing at least a few gorgeous outfits, so go ahead (it's part of the fun of preparing for a baby), but beyond that, try and stick to basics and see what gifts you get before buying half of Baby Gap.

Organic clothes are widely available. They're usually made of cotton, bamboo or wool produced without the use of pesticides. There's little firm evidence to suggest pesticides are harmful to babies but if you prefer to do your bit for the environment, by all means go organic. A bonus is that organic fabrics tend to be extra soft and aren't that much more expensive than good-quality standard cotton.

Look for...

- ***Washability*** If it can't be machine-washed and tumble-dried, walk away! That pure cashmere baby cardigan will get sick on it and hand-washing/trips to the dry cleaners are chores you won't welcome in the newborn weeks.
- ***Comfort*** Your mission as a new parent is to do almost anything to minimise your baby's crying and avoiding uncomfortable clothes (stiff fabrics and scratchy labels or seams, for example) is one small tactic in this battle against tears. Luckily you don't have to choose between comfort and style as there are some beautiful and comfy baby clothes around. Woven or jersey cotton and softest, thin denim are breathable and gentle against sensitive skin.
- ***Clothes that are easy to put on and take off*** Many babies dislike having clothes pulled over their heads and some parents feel a bit nervous about dressing their newborn, so look for tops with envelope necks, necks which open wider with poppers or wrap-over/kimono styles. Cardigans are better than sweaters and, faced with a wriggly baby, poppers and zips are easier to do up than buttons.
- ***Easy nappy access*** Nappy changing will be a key activity of your day, so go for easy-to-remove garments with poppers down the legs and avoid tights for girls until yours is older.

Clothing

£ Tesco, H&M, Boots • ££ Gap, Marks &Spencer, Zara, Next, John Lewis, Vertbaudet, Mothercare, Green Baby (✿) • £££ Timberland, Petit Bateau, Monsoon, Boden, The White Company

Some retailers use the term 'layette' for gift sets. Sometimes it simply means clothing for the early weeks, sometimes it includes bedding and sometimes bath towels as well.

❊ ***Shops with a good returns policy*** Nursery and baby clothing retailers tend to be generous about taking unwanted goods back and provided the items are unworn, many will exchange them or give vouchers for a similar sum even if you don't have a receipt. If you do have the receipt, some retailers will take things back long after they were purchased. So retain receipts, leave tags on until you know for sure you want to keep an item and don't rush into washing non-essentials before the birth.

Steer clear of...

❊ ***Clothes that could irritate or be dangerous for your baby*** This means avoiding garments made of scratchy synthetics or itchy lace, and those with big buttons, poorly finished seams or irritating labels. Check the underside of appliquéd decorations to ensure they are smoothly finished, skip collared shirts that come high up the neck, anything that does up at the back (hard to reach when your baby can't sit up and potentially uncomfortable if she is lying on the seam) and polyester (it can be clammy and irritating to delicate skin). Also avoid any garments with drawstrings longer than 15cm as these present a risk of strangulation.

❊ ***Buying lots in newborn/1 month size*** Unless you have a particularly small baby, these sizes will only fit for a few weeks. The average newborn weighs about 3.2 kilos (7 lb 11 oz) at birth, reaching around 4 kilos (10 lb) by four weeks. Small-sized clothes might not fit at all if you have an especially bruising baby. Buy a few newborn-size essentials and then mainly stick to the next size up; doing this is more

economical, although it might mean slightly baggy clothes for the first few weeks.

* *'Starter' sets of assorted clothing items* Not to be confused with multipacks (which are normally good value), you'll probably dislike or won't need some of the items in such sets, making them not as good a buy as they appear.

* *Snowsuits* Quilted all-in-ones look cosy but are impractical; as soon as you've managed to get your baby into one, sod's law says your baby's nappy will need changing and you'll have to take the whole thing off again! It's also easy for babies to overheat in these, especially if you're going in and out of shops, restaurants and the car. Since newborns don't tend to go running around in the snow, blankets, pram footmuffs (see page 119) and 'shaped fleece wraps' are more versatile ways to keep yours warm, given that these can be easily removed or opened-up when you go indoors.

* *Expensive baby shoes, hats, gloves and mittens* All are prone to getting lost.

☺☺ *Don't be tempted to scrimp on clothing. Given you'll have twice the babies and consequently half the time for laundry, you will definitely need double the amount of clothing.*

NEWBORN ESSENTIALS

SLEEPSUITS

Also called babygros, these are long-sleeved all-in-one outfits, typically made from stretchy jersey cotton, which are a mainstay for day as well as night wear in the first weeks. They're comfortable, cosy and needn't be pulled over a baby's floppy head. Those with integral 'feet' remove worries about socks dropping off — baby socks are notorious for this and also

getting lost in washing machines. (Sleepsuits with integral scratch mitts are practical for the same reason.)

Buy six newborn-size cotton jersey sleepsuits and six in the next size up. (Skip the newborn ones if you're expecting a big baby or don't mind your baby wearing slightly baggy clothing.)

Choose sleepsuits that do up with poppers down the front or side and the crotch/legs, and with integral 'feet'. Most department stores and large supermarkets offer reasonably priced multipacks.

SLEEPGOWNS

A practical alternative to sleepsuits for night-time, sleepgowns are like long nighties with elasticated bottoms that cover your baby's legs and feet. They make middle-of-the-night nappy changes easier because there's no fiddling with poppers; you just push the gown above your baby's waist and change away. They can be used under blankets or sleeping bags and as they're looser and don't have integral 'feet', are outgrown less quickly than sleepsuits. Some have integral scratch mitts. On the downside, unlike sleepsuits, they have to go over your baby's head when being put on and taken off (though most have envelope necks) and some people worry that little feet can get chilly in them (you can always use socks as well).

Buy one or two initially and see if you prefer them to sleepsuits for nightwear before buying more.

"I use short-sleeved bodysuits even for winter if they're going to be worn under another layer. I find longer sleeves can get ruffled underneath the outer layer and become uncomfortable."

●✚ *Once your baby is a few months old, you'll probably want to move on from sleepsuits in the daytime to 'proper' outfits.*

BODYSUITS

Also called vests, bodies or onesies, these are short- or long-sleeved tops that fasten at the crotch with poppers. They'll probably form a mainstay of your baby's wardrobe – worn under another top in cooler weather or alone in warmer months. They help keep nappies in place and don't ride up the way normal T-shirts do. If you're worried about pulling things over your baby's head, go for the wrap or 'kimono' style, which fastens at the side as well as underneath. Otherwise just ensure the necks are wide envelope ones or very stretchy.

Buy six to eight bodysuits in stretch cotton jersey in both newborn size and the next size up. Again, department stores and supermarkets sell good-value multipacks.

CARDIGANS OR HOODED, ZIPPED TOPS

Choose cotton rather than wool, which can be scratchy. If you do want to buy wool for winter, check it is non-irritating and can be machine washed. Tops should fasten with poppers or concealed zip closings instead of tiny buttons, which can be annoyingly fiddly. Buy two or three.

If a kind friend or relative offers to knit something for your baby, steer the knitter towards some of today's lovely, more modern patterns to avoid landing a dated woolly monstrosity.

SOCKS

Most baby socks are impossible to keep on. We might sound like an advert for Baby Gap but theirs really are the only ones we've found that reliably stay put. They also have non-slip soles so older, walking babies are less likely to slip on hard floors. If you do end up with a falling off socks problem, Sock-ons could help. They're inexpensive little elasticated straps that sit around the heel and instep, see www.sockons.co.uk.

Socks

Gap (especially their triple-cuffed socks); **Sock-ons**

Buy four pairs of socks; if you want to be really practical get them all in one colour, so that if some get lost the remainders make pairs.

◆ *Once your baby starts walking and needs shoes (see page 22), it's particularly important that her socks fit correctly. If they're too big, they can ruin a correctly fitted shoe by causing pressure; if they're too small, they could scrunch your baby's toes and inhibit correct foot growth. Pure cotton socks will minimise the possibility of fungal infection.*

HATS AND GLOVES

Hats shield your baby from harmful rays in summer and retain body heat in winter (babies haven't much hair to do the latter). Both summer and winter hats should be made from breathable fabrics such as cotton. Avoid brims that go all the way round for your newborn, who will spend most of her time lying on her back.

Mittens are preferable to gloves as they're easier to put on tiny hands.

Buy two hats appropriate to the season and for winter, two pairs of mittens.

●→ *Legionnaires' hats with back and side flaps offer extra protection for toddlers.*

SCRATCH MITTS

These tiny, inexpensive, cotton mittens stop newborns from scratching themselves with their sharp nails. Baby fingernails grow quickly and are tricky to cut, so if you have a 'scratchy' baby, these mitts are essential. Be warned: they have a tendency to get lost as they're so small. Look out for sleepsuits and sleepgowns with integral ones.

If you need to buy them separately, buy two pairs, then see if your baby is a scratcher before buying more.

Bear in mind that a sling or carrier counts as a layer of clothing, so be careful not to overdress your baby when using one. Your body warmth also will help keep him cosy. A rule of thumb for sling/carrier users is to dress your baby in as many layers as you dress yourself.

OTHER CLOTHING

For special occasions or when you get sick of the sight of sleepsuits, it's time to get some of those more interesting 'proper outfits' out of the wardrobe.

TROUSERS, LEGGINGS AND SHORTS

Soft, jersey material is the most practical choice for these, as it's comfy enough to stay on for daytime naps. Go for items with poppers for easy access to the nappy area or elasticated waists that are easy to pull up and down.

For more formal trousers, if your baby is slimmer than average, those with adjustable waistbands (try Next and M&S) will help overcome the dilemma of their either fitting at the waist and being too short, or fitting lengthwise but being too loose at the waist.

Buy four to six pairs of trousers for a boy but fewer for a girl if you're also splashing out on dresses and skirts.

●→ *Once your baby is being potty trained, babies of both sexes will need extra trousers, and girls skirts or dresses that can be easily taken on and off or lifted up and down.*

DRESSES AND SKIRTS

These are cool and pretty for a girl in summer (and super easy for nappy changing) but not so practical in winter when she'll have to wear them with tights, which can be a challenge to put on. Dresses are unnecessary for newborns, though, so either just buy a couple for special occasions or wait until your little girl is older. Trousers or leggings make better everyday winter wear.

T-SHIRTS

These can be worn over bodysuits as an extra, often more interesting layer. They can, of course, be worn without another top when the weather allows but because they tend to ride up exposing little tummies to the cold, for younger babies, we favour bodysuits instead. Look for t-shirts with stretchy necks or that open wide with buttons or press studs.

COATS

Your newborn can be kept warm with blankets, wraps or a footmuff or raincover when lying flat in her pram or buggy so doesn't really need a coat. However, a comfy little coat can be useful if you'll use a sling or carrier a lot.

Breathable polyurethane coated jackets with a fleece lining are our favoured option; the fleece adds warmth without bulk and the outer layer is showerproof. These are also pretty stain-resistant and easy to care for, so you should be able to manage with just buying one. If the lining is removable, even better, as you can then adjust the coat's warmth according to the weather. You might need to add an extra layer underneath this type of coat when the weather is very cold though, so err towards buying a slightly bigger size, to allow as well enough room for a cardigan.

"Babies and toddlers grow out of clothes so quickly we've found it worth watching out for bargains in the sales for the following year. By working out what size our children will be in the corresponding season next year, we can pick up some real bargains and designer stuff."

●✛ *Once your baby is sitting up in her pushchair, she'll need a winter coat. The ideal baby or toddler coat is lightweight and not so bulky that it hampers movement. Bear in mind that a very thick coat can compromise the safety of a car seat harness, which needs to fit relatively snugly on your baby.*

SHOES

Before your baby can walk properly, bootees and shoes are unnecessary and have an annoying tendency to fall off and get lost. That said, they look cute. If you're tempted, choose very soft ones which won't constrict your baby's foot growth.

● *Once she's walking, your baby will need her first pair of proper, outdoor shoes. We recommend getting shoes professionally fitted in a reputable shoe shop. Properly fitted shoes might cost a little more but a correct fit will prevent damage to growing feet. Clarks and John Lewis have trained fitters, as should independent children's shoe retailers – ask around for a local recommendation. Go for sturdy but flexible, low-cut shoes or trainers with an arch in the sole.*

BIBS

Newborn bibs are a godsend if your baby is the sicky type but you'll probably receive some as gifts, so don't buy too many in advance. Choose either the stretchy popover type that go over a baby's head or those with a side-fastening press stud; both are much easier to use than those that fasten at the back of the neck. Avoid tie-bibs completely and only get those with Velcro® fastenings if you can trust yourself to always fasten them before they go in the wash – otherwise that gorgeous designer outfit we advised you not to buy will come out of the washing machine stuck to the bib and ruined.

Bandana-style versions are a cooler, more attractive alternative to conventional bibs – almost a fashion accessory. There are plenty of these on the market now (search online for Dribble Ons, DribbleBusters or Skibz).

It's worth purchasing a few, as they'll need regular washing.

● *When teething (usually from around six months of age but it can be earlier or later), many babies dribble a lot. At this stage, you might find your baby needs a bib pretty much permanently attached to her neck.*

NAPPIES AND CHANGING ACCESSORIES

Clearly nappies will play a major part in your life for the next few years with much buying, changing and disposing/washing of them. Nappies and their contents will invade your shopping list, your thoughts and even your conversations. We guarantee you'll have a few chats about the contents of your baby's nappy or the staggering number of bowel movements she produces in a given day.

SHOPPING LIST

- ✓ Nappies
- ✓ Towelling squares
- ✓ Cottonwool pads and/or wipes
- ✓ Lidded nappy bin; if using washables you also need two laundry nets *or* a waterproof but washable drawstring laundry bag
- ✓ Nappy sacks
- ✓ Nappy cream
- ? Changing mat
- ✓ Changing bag or equivalent
- ✗ Nappy disposal unit
- ✗ Wipes warmer

For changing units see page 105.

You might not want to hear this – although we're going to tell you anyway – but a typical baby produces around 100 kilos of poo and 250 litres of wee in the first two-and-a-half years – thankfully not all at once. In fact, you'll be changing 5,000 or so nappies between your baby's birth and the time she graduates to the potty or loo.

THE GREAT WASHABLES VERSUS DISPOSABLES DEBATE

Even if you've never changed a nappy in your life, it'd be hard to have missed the arguments over whether disposables or washable/cloth nappies are the more environmentally friendly.

In the washables camp, you'll hear that disposables create huge amounts of landfill waste that takes decades to biodegrade and produces methane gas, contributing to global warming.

Cloth sceptics counter that laundering washables consumes copious water and energy, turning this supposedly eco-friendly option a rather paler shade of green.

Studies exist that support both views but many have been commissioned by interested parties with their own agendas. The UK's Environment Agency undertook perhaps the most comprehensive research, trying to get to the bottom (excuse the pun) of this tricky nappy debate. Their conclusion was that overall there's little difference between the environmental cost of the two types. Fans of 'cloth' claim this study was flawed as it assumed nappies weren't washed in the most eco-friendly manner. So for now it remains hard to know what the truth is and which way is best. And to complicate things further, you also need to consider...

THE MIDDLE GROUND (with less landfill in it)

Your choice isn't confined to creating huge amounts of landfill or gigantic loads of laundry, there's also a middle ground in the form of 'eco-disposables' (see page 34). These nappies offer the convenience of disposables but are at least partly biodegradable and have been manufactured with an eye on environmental issues, for example, without the use of chlorine and with reduced amounts of chemical gels. Of course, as a throwaway product, they use up resources in production and

NAPPY TYPES – A COMPARISON

	Washables	Standard disposables	Eco-disposables
Convenience for parents	Low *(storage and laundering needed)*	High	High
Landfill contribution	None	High	Lower if biodegradable
Energy and resources used in production	Low *(15 to 20 nappies are produced once and can be re-used for another baby)*	High *(at least 5,000 nappies for each child)*	Moderate to high *(eco-nappy manufacturing tends to be greener)*
Energy and resources used in laundering	Medium to high depending on temperature and drying method	None	None
Comfort for babies	Usually high *(soft cotton)*	Variable	Variable *(some brands are a bit scratchy and stiff)*
Absorbency and 'leak proofness'	Medium	High	Medium to high
Initial cost	High	Low	Low
Ongoing cost	Low *(laundering costs only)*	High	High
Total cost *(estimate assuming 5,000 nappy changes)*	£350–450	£650–750	£950–1000

Unless you're insistent on using cloth all the time, it's usually more convenient to start with eco- or standard disposables for at least the first few days post birth, before switching over. Even later on, it needn't be a black-and-white decision; you may want to deploy the odd disposable when travelling or on a long day out.

Don't cough up for a full set of washables before testing them out. Get trial packs and see if cloth is really for you and which brand you like; brands vary a lot in absorbency, ease of use and fit (some are better for chubby babies, others for slimmer ones).

transportation and the methane problem remains, but they are still more eco-friendly than standard disposables.

So, which way to go?

Until the washable or disposable debate is put to bed (which at this rate could take as long as the biodegradation of a disposable nappy), it's down to you to decide which route works best for your new family. Issues to consider include convenience, eco-friendliness, comfort, absorbency and cost.

WASHABLE OR CLOTH NAPPIES

Today's cloth nappies come in different versions and may have several components (see chart on the opposite page). Terry nappies, a mainstay of previous generations, are still available as cheaper cloth options. If you add a flushable liner to catch 'solids', it makes the cleaning process less grim.

Washables do cost more to buy initially but they're cheaper than disposables in the long run, and some local authorities offer free trial packs or subsidies to help get you started with them. You can also use them for more than one child or sell them once they're no longer needed (believe it or not there's strong demand for secondhand nappies). Flat cloth nappies also can double as dribble cloths and bibs, as camouflage when breastfeeding or as an improvised sun shade for the pushchair or cover for a changing mat.

The challenge is choosing between the different 'systems'. However, there are some excellent cloth nappy specialists online who can advise further on specific types. If choosing cloth nappies, bear the following pluses and minuses in mind:

+ Soft on sensitive skin.
+ Babies in washables tend to potty train more easily as they understand 'being wet'.
− Can be inconvenient when travelling as you need to take dirty nappies home when out, rather than throwing them away.
− Bulky; clothes can be too tight in nappy area.

CLOTH NAPPY KNOW-HOW

COMPONENTS:

❉ *Wrap or outer:* waterproof layer that sits on top of the nappy inner to hold in moisture.

❉ *Nappy/inner:* soft, absorbent layer which soaks up wee and runnier poo. Can be separate or integrated with a wrap or outer.

❉ *Flat nappy:* a basic type of nappy inner which is a muslin or towelling square you need to fold yourself.

❉ *Pre-fold:* similar to a flat nappy inner but with a pre-folded thicker section.

❉ *Shaped nappy:* a nappy inner that is shaped like a disposable nappy – no folding required.

❉ *Liner:* an extra washable cloth or flushable layer, which makes disposing of nappy contents easier.

❉ *Pocket:* an opening, which you can stuff with a shaped or folded inner or booster for absorbency.

❉ *Booster:* an additional pad which can be put in a nappy to add absorbency if needed, particularly at night time.

TYPES:

❉ *Two-piece/separate:* the inner and wrap layers aren't attached.

❉ *All-in-one:* the inner and wrap layers are sewn together for ease of use.

❉ *All-in-two:* the inner and wrap layers can be attached together – usually via poppers, but separate for washing and quicker drying.

❉ *One-size/birth to potty:* a nappy system which is adjustable for all sizes of baby from birth to potty training.

❉ *Sized:* a nappy that comes in different sizes for differently aged babies.

THE MAIN BUYING DECISIONS
Which style of cloth nappy to go for?

Broadly speaking there are five types of washable nappy: flat/pre-fold and shaped, which require a wrap; all-in-one, all-in-two and pocket (for more info, see chart overleaf).

Verdict: We favour all-in-twos as they offer the best of both worlds: they come apart for quick drying but are fastened together for ease of getting them onto your baby or toddler.

CLOTH NAPPY TYPES

DESCRIPTION

Two piece with standard nappy insert and separate wrap	The nappy has two layers, which are put on separately: a traditional terry or muslin square that is either flat or has a thicker panel stitched in (pre-folds). Flats are fastened with pins or 'nappi nippas' and both types need covering with a waterproof wrap.
Two piece with shaped nappy plus separate wrap	The inner is shaped like a disposable and goes under a waterproof wrap.
All-in-one	A waterproof outer layer with an integral absorbent inner, shaped like a disposable nappy.
All-in-two	Shaped nappies having a wrap and nappy inner that popper together to form an all-in-one but which can be separated for washing or drying.
Pocket nappy systems	Shaped nappies with a combined waterproof outer layer and softer inner layer and a pocket to which you add absorbent material..

PROS	CONS	COST
• Cheap. • Widely available. • Not as bulky as other types and can be folded to fit all shapes of baby. • Quick drying. • Flats are one size so no need to upgrade to bigger ones later (although you may need to buy sized wraps).	• Fiddly to use. • Can be troublesome for any babysitters who aren't used to them.	£
• Easy to wash. • No folding required.	• Can be bulky *(especially one-size versions)*. • Easier to use than flats but more fiddly than all-in-ones.	££
• Easy to put on your baby *(so especially good for child carers or nursery)*.	• Take longer to dry as thicker. • Wear out quicker as the whole thing needs washing after each use (separate wraps may not need so much washing). • Less absorbent and not too good at containing leaks. • Expensive.	£££
• Easy to get onto your baby once pre-assembled (you simply fasten the inner and outer layers together). • As fast drying as two pieces. • No folding required. • Relatively slim fitting.	• Fiddlier than all-in-ones as they require 'reassembling'. • Expensive.	£££
• Can control absorbency by using different 'stuffing' in the pocket. • Fast drying as come apart. • No folding required. • Relatively slim fitting.	• More fiddly than all-in-ones as they require 'stuffing'.	££

Boring they might be but towelling squares are nonetheless fab and have a multitude of uses, from lining changing mats to nappies for cloth users. We recommend getting six towelling squares. This sounds a lot but they're cheap and long lasting.

Washables
TotsBots Easyfit, The Pop-in Nappy System

Motherease,
Bambino Mio

Which fabric?

Inner layers are usually made from cotton, fleece, bamboo or hemp cloth. Which you choose is a matter of personal preference but inners should feel soft and absorbent (see our star buys for strong-performing brands).

Sized or one-size-fits-all nappies?

Some washable nappies come in different sizes; others are adjustable and designed to fit from birth to potty training age.

Sized versions fit better throughout, especially if your baby is particularly slim, chubby or a late potty trainer, but you will have to buy a new set once or twice as your baby grows.

One-size-fits-all nappies generally work out cheaper. Which type will be right for your depends on your priority of cost versus fit.

Verdict: Invest in sized nappies if you can afford them. They fit newborns better and are less likely to leak. They're a sensible buy if you plan more than one child as wear and tear will be less than with a one-size nappy. If you're a late switcher from disposables to cloth, you should find the birth-to-potty versions adequate.

How many?

This partly depends on how often you're willing to do a wash. Assuming you wash on alternate days and line or air dry rather than tumble dry, you should buy 18 to 20 nappies, be they nappy inserts for two-pieces or all-in-ones. For two-piece nappy systems, four wraps should suffice as unless they're soiled, they needn't be washed after every nappy change.

WRAPS

Wraps and outer layers, required for two-piece systems, are typically made from polyester fleece or coated cotton or wool. They need to be waterproof but quick drying and feel relatively soft, rather than stiff or crinkly, against your baby's skin.

Look for...

❉ *Fit and sizing that works for your baby* Some brands are better for slimmer babies and others for chubbier ones; it may take some trial and error to find the right one for your baby. FuzziBunz Elite are especially adjustable to fit varying sizes of baby round both the waist and legs.

❉ *Absorbency* Leaky nappies can wake a baby up at night so choose fabric that's particularly absorbent (microfibre, hemp and bamboo tend to be better than cotton) or brands where you can add a booster pad if needed for night time.

❉ *Drying time and method* Some wraps can't be tumble dried so you'll have to avoid these if that's your preferred drying method (not very eco-friendly). Some materials dry quicker than others – fleece is a good, fast-drying choice. All-in-ones take longer to dry so you might need to buy more.

❉ *Wraps/outers that are breathable* A breathable wrap will help prevent nappy rash and keep your baby cool in hot weather. PUL is better than plastic or PVC coatings for breathability.

❉ *Fastening method* Velcro® is faster to do up than poppers but tends to get caught on other items in the laundry. Nappies that tie on are annoying to do up so avoid them.

❉ *The cost from birth to potty training* If possible, try to focus on this rather than the initial outlay.

WASHING CLOTH NAPPIES

Some local councils and companies run nappy laundering services. Their eco-credentials are debatable, however. Although 'commercial' washing methods are probably greener, the collection and delivery mileage clocked up also has to be taken into consideration. A laundering service will provide you with freshly washed nappies each week and take away used ones. You still need to purchase and wash the wraps yourself.

If you launder at home, and the majority of cloth users do, ideally skip the tumble drier. Using an eco-friendly laundry liquid/powder or a detergent alternative such as 'eco-balls' can also help keep things greener. See below for advice on storing dirty nappies before washing them.

Cloth nappies are bulkier than disposables so you might need to buy clothes one size larger to accommodate the nappy. Frugi's clothing range isn't cheap but is specifically 'cut for cloth', i.e. designed to fit over washables.

NAPPY LINERS AND BOOSTERS

Adding a liner to washable nappies helps keep a baby's skin drier and makes it easier to dispose of poo. Liners can be washable or disposable (these should be biodegradable and flushable).

You can also buy booster pads (typically fleece or towelling) to add extra absorbency for night time, or alternatively use a folded muslin or towelling square. Some nappy systems offer booster pads as part of the package.

STANDARD DISPOSABLES

Disposable nappies are undeniably convenient and are used by the vast majority of parents. However, your outside bin quickly fills up with them, which can be problematic for those with fortnightly refuse collections or who have more than one child in nappies.

"We used disposables for the first few hectic weeks but switched to washables once everything calmed down a bit. If we're away we still use disposables, although we try to stick to the greener brands."

Most contain a material called polyacrylate, which when wet becomes a gel, absorbing many times its own weight in liquid. Some also have a stay-dry layer rather like on sanitary towels.

The best-known brands are Pampers and Huggies, although supermarket and other own-label brands can be cheaper and often perform just as well. The absorbency, bulkiness, fit and softness of nappy brands do vary, so try different ones and see which you prefer and which fit your baby best.

Look for...

❋ *Cost per nappy* Different brands come in different-sized packs, making price comparisons tricky; some supermarkets display a price per nappy, which is more useful (newborn nappies tend to cost from 11 to 16p each). There will almost always be one brand on offer in supermarkets, so you could swap and change if money is tight or stock up when your favoured brand is discounted (don't overstock as your baby will need different sizes and possibly styles as she grows). Bigger packs save money; nappies in larger economy packs cost around 25% less per nappy than those in small packs.

❋ *A good fit* As with cloth nappies, some will suit your baby's shape better than others. Larger gaps around the thighs and top could mean leaks.

❋ *Lack of bulkiness* Once your baby starts getting mobile, a bulky nappy can annoy her and hamper movement.

❋ *Softness* Some brands are a bit scratchy around the edges and this can irritate sensitive skin.

❋ *The right 'stage' nappy for your baby* Newborn nappies are designed to absorb and hold in the runnier poo new babies produce, whereas nappies for older babies offer greater flexibility and stretchiness for crawlers and walkers.

❋ *Size* Look at the weight range and move to the next size when your baby reaches the relevant minimum weight; the bigger size will offer more absorbency.

How many?

Newborns can get through 12 nappies a day, although more typically eight. Older babies might only need four to six.

❋ **Disposables**
For newborns: Aldi Mamia, Pampers, Tesco Baby Newborn •
For older babies: Aldi Mamia, Pampers, Lidl Toujours, Huggies

- -

PRODUCT SHOWCASE

Aldi's 'Mamia' own-brand nappies and Lidl's 'Toujours' range are surprisingly good and very well priced. We know many converts; they are definitely worth checking out. Note that at the time of writing Lidl don't do a newborn size, so you will have to wait some weeks until your baby is big enough for their smallest size.

- -

Eco Disposables
Bambo, Moltex

ECO-DISPOSABLES

Unfortunately, eco-disposables aren't that widely available. The Nature brand can be found in some supermarkets, Boots and Mothercare, but others such as Moltex, Tushies Gel and Bambo are mainly sold online or in specialist 'greener' nursery shops and some health-food stores. Add to this that most eco-disposables are more expensive and some don't perform as well as mainstream brands (they are usually bulkier) and this could explain why their use isn't more commonplace.

Of the eco-disposable options on the market, Bambo and Moltex get more positive feedback from parents than the better-known and more widely sold Nature range. Both Bambo and Moltex are soft, absorbent and slim-fitting although they might cost a few pence more than Pampers per nappy. It's worth getting trial packs of several brands to see which you like best.

If you do go for a cartridge-based nappy disposal unit, reduce spending on refills by confining use to poo-filled nappies and putting wee-only ones (which don't smell) in your regular bin.

Verdict: Despite question marks over how biodegradable some eco-disposables really are, these are a good compromise for those whose conscience is troubled by standard disposables.

CHANGING ACCESSORIES

NAPPY DISPOSAL

Disposables will end up in your refuse bin sooner or later but if you don't want to traipse outside after each and every change, you have two options.

Firstly, a nappy disposal unit. This wraps the nappy and its contents and stores them in a relatively odour-proof (and toddler-proof) bin, which only needs emptying when full.

Second;y, a standard lidded nappy pail. Used nappies are placed in scented sacks first, to mask smells a little and ensure you don't have to clean the pail too often.

Be aware that nappy disposal units require refill cartridges; the bins themselves are relatively cheap but you will be shelling out for cartridges for a couple of years. Although basic nappy pails need emptying more frequently to prevent the pong getting too bad, they work out a lot cheaper.

Regardless of what you do at home, you'll need a small stash of nappy sacks in your changing bag, for when you're out. They don't cost a lot and are handy for all sorts of other uses, like storing wet bathing suits after swimming or soiled items during toilet training, or as makeshift rubbish bags in the car.

Verdict: A standard cheap nappy pail plus sacks works fine if you don't mind more frequent bin emptying; you'll probably need to do it at least daily, more in hot weather.

NAPPY STORAGE
Dirty nappies Used cloth nappies are best stored in either a mesh nappy bag within a lidded nappy pail or in a large waterproof, drawstring laundry bag (many washable nappy specialist websites sell these in their accessories sections). On wash day, you simply turn the mesh or laundry bag with its contents inside out while loading it into your washing machine.

You can store the nappies in the bag or pail 'dry', or add nappy soak or tea tree oil. You'll need to buy a second mesh or laundry bag for when the other one is in the wash.

When you're out and about, a smaller waterproof, sealable bag is useful for bringing soiled washable nappies home in or you could use biodegradable nappy sacks.

Clean nappies You can buy fabric nappy storage units for clean nappies (sometimes called 'nappy stackers') but these aren't necessary and most parents just keep disposables in the packaging and washables in a drawer, or on a shelf near their changing mat.

WIPES
Wipes come in unscented, scented, biodegradable and 'natural' varieties. Midwives tend to recommend starting with cottonwool (pads are more practical for wiping than balls) and water instead of wipes, as this is gentler for newborn skin. Wipes are, however, much more convenient, especially when out, and most parents find those that are for sensitive skin or contain only natural ingredients (see our product showcase

You can avoid or cut down on the use of disposable wipes by making washable ones; fleece or terry fabric are good for nappy changes. Some ready-made kits are also available; these include wipes, essential oils and storage tubs.

Wipes
Disposable: Jackson **Reece Kinder by Nature, WaterWipes** (especially good for newborns)
Washable: **Cheeky Wipes**

Wipes dry out easily and the supposedly stay-shut sticky lids don't tend to. Store the packet upside down to prevent drying or look out for free storage tubs with jumbo packs.

Nappy Creams
Standard: Sudocrem, Metanium · ✿ Green Baby Nappy Balm, Neal's Yard, Little Green Sheep Nappy Balm, Earth Friendly Baby Red Clover

below for an example) are fine even for delicate skin. Fragrance is certainly best avoided – and indeed unnecessary.

Wipes vary in price but there will almost always be one brand on offer in any given store – so if you have a favourite, stock up when it's discounted.

When going out, decant wipes into a small wipes holder (included with some changing bags) or a re-sealable freezer bag. This saves carrying a full heavy pack of wipes around or paying more for the slim-line travel packs.

WIPES WARMERS

Despite their popularity in the US, many British parents are unimpressed. Some babies hate cold wipes but most tolerate them, especially if they don't know any different. Generally warmers are a faff and extra expense you can do without. Only consider if your baby consistently squeals at cold wipes.

NAPPY CREAM

Specially formulated creams treat and prevent nappy rash. You probably won't need to use one all the time unless your baby's bottom is especially susceptible to rashes.

Sudocrem and Metanium act as barriers but are also good for treatment once a rash occurs. Earth Friendly Baby Red Clover has more portable packaging, so its's best for your changing bag.

PRODUCT SHOWCASE

DermaH$_2$O WaterWipes have been developed with worries about standard wipes irritating newborn skin in mind and are becoming a popular alternative to cottonwool and water. They're impregnated with 99.9% water and 0.1% fruit juice and no chemicals or stronger oils; most parents we know who've tried them on their baby's bottom have been very impressed. They are, however, more expensive than most other brands so you could perhaps use these for the first few months and then switch to cheaper ones later if you are confident by then that your baby's skin isn't prone to irritation.

PRODUCT SHOWCASE

Sudocrem is a staple both during and beyond children's nappy years. Use it for everything from rubbing on cuts and grazes (it's an antiseptic) to soothing sunburn in summer and treating your own chapped skin in winter (parental hands also can get sore from all the post nappy-change hand washing).

CHANGING MATS

You can use a large towel under your baby but mats are inexpensive and make a comfortable, easy-to-clean surface.

Standard A changing mat should consist of a large cushioned pad with a washable or wipeable waterproof cover. Some are plain and functional; others have decidedly funky coverings. Most come with slightly raised sides but these have limited use when it comes to the somewhat impossible challenge of keeping mobile older babies in place at changing time.

Waterproof vinyl is more practical than towelling and you can line it with a muslin, towelling square or towel to make it less of a cold shock for your baby's bottom.

Portable When you're away from home, you'll also need something on which to change your baby; most changing bags come with a mat included but if yours doesn't, a quick online

✳ Changing Mats
£ John Lewis own brand mats, Mothercare Wedge-shaped Changing Mat •
££ ZPM Multimats (attractive designs, wipeable on one side, soft cotton on the other), **East Coast Changing Mat with Play Arch**

PRODUCT SHOWCASE

Pampers or **Babytec Disposable Change Mats** Disposable changing mats are extremely useful when out and about. While not terribly eco-friendly they're not as bad as they sound, as they can be reused many times. Their great benefit is, if they do get soiled or used on a really grubby changing unit when you're out (and believe us some of these are revolting), you can just chuck them away, rather than carting a horrible mat back home to be cleaned up. They're lighter and more compact than most travel mats (although rather less padded), and can double as protection when potty training.

Once your baby becomes more active, use distraction to encourage cooperation at changing time. Keep an interesting toy only for nappy changes or invest in a wall-mountable mobile.

search for 'travel changing mat' will bring up lots of inexpensive options.

CHANGING BAGS

These purpose-designed bags, also sometimes known as nappy bags, are great for dragging around the endless amounts of kit you'll need to take with you whenever you go out with your baby. They aren't essential, as you could make do with a regular bag and add a compact changing pouch (see page 39), but most proper changing bags have plenty of features designed to make organising baby essentials easier.

Changing bags used to be dull, functional affairs and indeed there are still some boring ones on the market, but there are also lots of gorgeous, covetable versions that wouldn't be out of place on a catwalk (and not all with designer price tags). Styles include rucksacks, messenger bags (popular with dads), ones that fit over pram handles and extra-large models for twins. Most include a changing mat and some a bottle insulator/holder but if the one you want doesn't, these can be added separately. Although practicalities are important, choose a style and a design you like, because you could be carrying this one bag around for the next two years or more.

Verdict: Styles and designs are a personal thing but remember there's no need to settle for dull (unless that's what you want). Go beyond the high street to find more original designs.

✳ **Changing Bag**
£ Minene • ££ Pacapod • £££ Storksak

✳ £ BabyMel • ££ Skiphop • ££ to £££ OiOi • £££ Pink Lining, il Tutto

Look for...
✻ *A wipeable interior and exterior.*
✻ *Several pockets* These should separate feeding and nappy-changing stuff, keep bottles or food jars upright and help you find things easily (although conversely too many pockets defeats the object).
✻ *An integral changing mat* If included, it should be large enough for an older baby to lie on, easy to wipe down or wash, and have some padding to keep your baby comfortable if she's being changed on a hard surface. Changing mats can be bought separately.

WHAT TO PUT IN YOUR CHANGING BAG

- ✓ Nappies
- ✓ Wipes
- ✓ Nappy cream
- ✓ Nappy sacks/waterproof bag for washables
- ✓ Portable changing mat
- ✓ Muslins
- ✓ Bibs
- ✓ Spare clothes for your baby (vest and sleepsuit)
- ✓ Dummies (if using them)
- ✓ Bottle and formula dispenser (unless breastfeeding)
- ✓ A favourite toy/teether
- ✓ Hand sanitising gel
- ✓ Spare top for you if your baby is the sicky type

❋ ***A design suitable for others who will use the bag*** It shouldn't offend; if Dad's going to carry the bag, too, a girly floral print might be unwise.

❋ ***Decent capacity*** Like it or not, you'll need something big. There's a lot to go in there – spare clothes, bottles, snacks, nappies, wipes, changing mat, toys, kitchen sink...

PORTABLE CHANGING POUCHES

If you don't want a dedicated changing bag, you can buy handy little pouches to use in any bag. They open out into a mat, hold two or three nappies and have a compartment in which to keep wipes.

Portable Changing Pouch First Years Fold and Go, Melobaby

OiOi Compact Mat, Skip Hop Pronto

CHAPTER 3

BATHS, TOILETRIES AND GROOMING GEAR

BATHING

Bathing a newborn the first few times can be daunting, with you juggling a slippery and possibly screaming baby, washing his nooks and crannies, calming him and grabbing sponges and

---

SHOPPING LIST

- ✓ Bath support or baby bath with integral support
- ✓ Soft towel solely for your baby's use
- ✓ Flannel or sponge
- ✓ Baby nail clippers or scissors
- ✓ Hairbrush
- ? Baby bath
- ? Baby bath stand *(only if you have a bad back)*
- ? Bath ring *(for use from around six months)*
- ? Bath thermometer
- ? Toiletries
- ✗ Travel baby baths *(unless you'll stay somewhere without a normal bath)*
- ✗ Bath dressers
- ✗ Bath 'sets' *(such as a baby bath plus towel, top and tail bowl, toiletries)*
- ✗ Top and tail bowls

a towel. At moments like this, you wonder why we don't have more hands! But never fear, the baby products industry did invent a few useful products, which make this whole 'ordeal' more manageable.

YOU COULD USE THE KITCHEN SINK BUT...

Yes, you can bath babies in the kitchen sink but if you're anything like us, especially when we had newborns, your sink will be way too full of dirty dishes to fit a Barbie doll in, never mind a baby. If you are more domesticated than we are (and that's not difficult), a large kitchen sink makes a good first bath. It can certainly be easier on your back as there's no bending over the bath's side as you lift your baby in and out and hold him while he's in there. But doing this will require you to drag all your bath-time stuff downstairs and we find most people prefer to stick to the bathroom these days.

Whether you use the sink, the family bath or a baby bath, the challenge is in keeping a hand under your newborn – who after all won't be able to support his own head, let alone sit up – and managing to wash him, then grabbing the towel at the end. So what you need is a way to prop your baby up and keep his head out of the water.

The major options

❋ Buy a baby bath with an integral support or a bucket-style bath, which lets your baby sit up; this means you have to buy and store only one item.
❋ Buy a bath support and use this in your main bath; this takes up less space in the bathroom but needs more water, and takes more time to fill.
❋ Buy both a bath support and a standard baby bath; the smaller bath takes less time and water to fill and your baby will be supported, but you have the costs of buying two pieces of kit and have to store them both.

BABY BATHS

A small baby bath, while quicker to fill and using less water than your family one, will take up room in your bathroom if you store it there. Moreover, other than a few exceptions (the

Tippitoes Mini-bath and the Mamas & Papas Acqua Ergo Bath), most still don't solve the problem of supporting your baby.

If you do want a baby bath, they're well suited to being bought secondhand or borrowed. There are two main types.

Standard These cheap (around £6 to £20), scaled-down baths are sometimes cheerfully decorated with cute or hideous (depending on your taste) character motifs. They can be used until your baby is around six months old, but unless you're happy to hold him with both hands, you'll need to choose one with an integral support or add a separate support (see below).

Look for...
❉ *An integral support.*
❉ *A sturdy plastic construction.*
❉ *A non-slip base.*
❉ *Easy-to-grip handles or sides* if you'll need to move the bath between rooms when it's full of water.

Bucket More compact than standard baby baths, these are essentially purpose-designed plastic buckets, which allow a baby to sit snugly in a familiar fetal position during bathing. Note that you will need to hold your newborn's head when he is in the tub so although they're more supportive than standard baby baths, they don't allow you to be totally hands free, and you can't use a bath support in one.

Standard Bath
Tippitoes Mini-bath;
Mamas & Papas Acqua
Ergo

Bucket Bath
Tummytub, Mebby
Cocoon

PRODUCT SHOWCASE

The **Tippitoes Mini-bath** has an integral support and is impressive value at less than £15. It's compact – making it easy to store, fill and empty – yet large enough to last until your little one is ready for the main tub. Another option is the **Mamas & Papas Acqua Ergo** bath which features two integral supports – one for younger babies and another for older ones who are just learning to sit. However, unlike the 'mini' Tippitoes one, this is a full-size baby bath so will take up more space and it's more expensive.

+ Comforting and soothing for babies as sitting in a fetal position surrounded by warm water is a throwback to being in the womb.
+ They're compact – good for travel.
+ Much easier to move between rooms when filled than regular baby baths.
+ Use less water.
− More expensive.
− Getting the baby in and out can be awkward at first.
− You'll need to keep a hand on a young baby.
− No room for older babies to play and splash about although those used to these won't know what they're missing and tend to want to stay in them as long as possible.

A bucket bath will probably either appeal to you or not. If you do get one, it might take a while to master using it, but it will be worth persevering. Although they're recommended for babies up to eight months, we know of older ones who still like going in theirs.

Verdict: The **Tippitoes Mini-bath** with integral support is hard to beat unless you've a bad back (see tip, right). If you're having twins, go for two supports in the main bath.

BATH SUPPORTS

Also called a bath seat or sling, a bath support is akin to a mini-lounger, on which your little one lies within the main or baby bath. Designed for younger babies to use until they can sit up (which usually happens at about age six to ten months), a support lifts your baby's head clear of the water, so you don't have to keep a hand under him, leaving you freer to wash him and grab the towel at the end. Supports are cheap to buy and can easily be bought secondhand or borrowed. Note that you won't be able to use a support in a bucket-style bath. If you use a small, standard baby bath, make sure the support will fit in it (it might be wise to purchase both items in the same shop so you can check).

If you have a bad back, or have had a caesarean and struggle to bend over the side of the family bath or get comfortable beside a baby bath on the floor, you need to raise the bath to a more convenient height. Mothercare's Supabath rests of on the rim of your main tub. However, it does still require some bending and you'll need to ensure it will fit on your bath. If even reaching down into this will be a strain, consider a baby bath with a stand (the Tippitoes Mini-bath has an optional stand) although this adds to the expense and isn't easy to fill and empty.

"When Isabella was on the bath support I worried she'd get cold as the water wasn't covering her, so we'd put a wet flannel over her and pour warm water on to it to keep her warmer."

Types of bath support

✳ *Foam/sponge* Firm but soft, these slab-like supports usually have a central baby-shaped indentation.

+ Probably the comfiest option for your baby.
− Can become mildewed and you'll have to remember to wring it out, and even then it can still get a bit whiffy.
− Some compact down too much under the weight of your baby so they won't raise him out of the water sufficiently, which, in our view, rather defeats the purpose.

✳ *Fabric* Sometimes also called bath slings or hammocks, these range from a simple frame with towelling stretched across it to fancy bath 'chairs' with little head pillows.

+ Comfortable and practical.
− May become mildewed, unless the cover is machine washable.
− You might need to keep a hand hovering by your baby to stop him slipping off.

✳ *Moulded plastic* Although made of hard plastic, these supports are contoured so they 'fit' a baby's shape.

+ Support your baby well.
+ Easy to clean, so definitely the most practical.
− Can feel hard but you could always add a flannel on the top to soften the surface.

✳ **Moulded Bath Support**
Jahgoo, Emmay

Verdict: Due to the high praise they receive from parents, it would seem that babies are comfy enough in moulded plastic supports so, if you want to get a separate support, we definitely favour these.

OTHER BATH-TIME ITEMS

INFLATABLE AND FOLDING BABY BATHS

These are marketed as useful for travel and small bathrooms in which parents might struggle to store a normal baby bath. However, if you do have a small bathroom, you are probably better off with a bath support in the main tub, which won't be that bulky anyway. If you don't have a bath at all, the Flexibath packs flat, and can be used as a toy box or laundry basket later on. Its sides are quite steep and therefore not that supportive but there's the option of adding a support.

When you are away from home for a few days, it will be cheaper and easier to use a normal bath at your destination (unless you've already bought a folding bath), or to carry your baby into the shower with you or to manage by simply topping and tailing.

BATH DRESSERS

These are changing unit/bath combinations with shelves underneath and a bath usually hidden under a detachable changing tray. Unless you have a serious back problem and can't bend over even to use a rest-on-rim bath, please, please

☺☺ *When bathing two babies at once, your best bet is to get two moulded plastic supports and use them in the main bath. Since they free up your hands, they're the only feasible way for one person to manage twin bath times.*

Folding Bath
Flexibath

avoid wasting money on one. They're expensive, usually quite ugly, take up a lot of space and the bath's useful life is short. You must either carry a bath heavy with water to the dresser or fill it with jugs of water, which is tiresome; either way there's a good chance you'll slosh water everywhere.

If you do feel the need to buy one, those with a pipe can at least be emptied directly into your sink or bath (it won't help with the filling).

BATH STANDS

These enable you to rest a baby bath securely on top and are designed to save you from kneeling bath side. As with dressers, you still have to lift a heavy bath full of water on and off, which will challenge your back muscles, or fill and empty the bath with a jug, which will be a faff. Moreover, one will be an extra item to pay for and store. Generally, for these reasons, we only recommend them if you have a bad back; the Tippitoes Mini-bath has an optional folding stand.

●✚ *Once your baby is around six months old and has outgrown his bath support, you might want to consider a bath ring (also known as a bath seat). This is a plastic seat with a ring around the edge that supports older babies, allowing them to sit up in the bath without toppling over. Most are awkward to lift your baby in and out of and aren't useful for long, as your baby will soon be able to sit unsupported on a non-slip bathmat.*

Verdict: Generally, we think these aren't worth buying; borrow one or manage without, but if you do feel the need to get one, the Jane Fluid Foldable Bath Ring opens at the front making it easier to get your baby into the seat.

BABY TOWELS

✦ Baby Towels
Cuddledry

Special baby towels with hoods (sometimes called 'cuddle robes') look cute but all too many of them are made of disappointingly thin terry towelling so lack absorbency and cosiness, and tend to be so small that your baby will need a bigger towel within a few months. In our opinion, they aren't worth buying. Any normal soft towel for your baby's exclusive

PRODUCT SHOWCASE

Cuddledry towels fasten around your neck leaving your hands free to lift your baby out of the bath, thereby avoiding that tricky moment where you must hold the towel and simultaneously grab your baby (hoping that if you drop anything it's the towel). They're quite expensive (£25 to £30 each) but make a real difference if you often manage bath time alone. Made from wonderfully thick, soft, organic towelling, they're also generously sized so will last through to toddlerhood. One should suffice as you can manage with a normal towel when the Cuddledry is being washed. **Clevermama** do something similar, which is a little cheaper but the fabric isn't quite so cosy in our view.

use will do. However, if you really want to invest in a special baby towel, then the large apron-style baby towels, such as those made by Cuddledry – see product showcase above – are an exception.

Verdict: Manage without and just use a standard soft towel. (In any event, you might receive one or two hooded towels as baby gifts.)

FLANNEL OR SPONGE
You also need to have a flannel or sponge (natural ones are particularly soft) exclusively for your baby's use. Unlike towels, purpose-made ones for baby are recommended as they are softer on a baby's skin.

BATH THERMOMETERS
The time-honoured technique of dunking your elbow in the bath to check that the water temperature is suitable (it should feel pleasantly warm, not hot) means that a bath thermometer isn't a necessity. If you do feel the need to get one, we recommend those that can also be used as room thermometers as you'll get more use out of them.

✳ **Bath Thermometer**
Brother Max Ray Digital
Bath and Room
Thermometer

TOP AND TAIL BOWLS

These are plastic bowls, split into two sections to separate the water for wiping a baby's face and bottom in the early weeks when daily baths aren't necessary. They're cheap (£3 to £5) but entirely pointless when any two ordinary clean bowls will do, plus you'll probably only top and tail for a short period before more frequent baths and baby wipes take over.

Verdict: A complete waste of cash!

Toiletries
Littleme

££ Weleda Baby, Burt's Bees, Earth Friendly Baby, Green Baby, Little Green Sheep

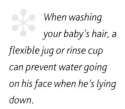

When washing your baby's hair, a flexible jug or rinse cup can prevent water going on his face when he's lying down.

BATHING 'SETS'

Some retailers sell bundles of bathing items including perhaps a baby bath, bath thermometer, towel and top and tail bowl, sometimes decorated with a theme. These probably won't save you money unless you want or need all the items and they rarely contain the best products of each type anyway.

TOILETRIES

Rewind a few decades and most new mums brandished bottles of baby bath, baby lotion and talc aplenty. Nowadays there's more of a 'back-to-basics' approach since many parents worry about using chemical ingredients. In fact, many midwives advise that plain water is perfectly adequate for newborn bathing and that olive oil is one of the best, most natural ways to moisturise baby skin. Moreover, talcum powder has been thrown out with the baby's bath water; studies have shown even small amounts can be harmful if inhaled and besides, with modern nappies and a decent nappy cream, it isn't needed.

When it comes to shampoos, newborn hair rarely needs washing and even that of older babies only needs it infrequently. This is a very good thing because most little people aren't exactly ecstatic about having it done and many scream through the process. Some shampoos seem to sting eyes more than others but when it comes to that 'no more tears' claim of a well-known brand, there isn't a shampoo around that can solve the problem of babies hating their faces being drenched with water.

If and when you want to introduce lotions and potions for your baby, there are plenty of organic and natural ranges,

although they tend to cost a bit more than the likes of Johnson's. A look at the lengthy lists of chemical ingredients on the back of most standard baby toiletries can be a convincing argument that it's worth paying the extra to go organic.

●→ *If your older baby gets upset having his hair washed, once he's able to sit up in the bath, a visor can stop water getting on his face and might prevent tears at bath time.*

GROOMING GEAR

NAIL CLIPPERS AND SCISSORS

Tiny nails grow remarkably quickly and are challenging to cut when junior is wriggling about (our best baby manicure tip is to do it when he's asleep). Some people find little nail clippers easier, others prefer round-ended baby nail scissors – there's no right answer so choose whichever you prefer. A few parents gently nibble or bite their baby's fingernails when they're newborn and their nails are soft (this is easier after they've had a bath). Whichever method you go with, a small emery board can be useful to smooth off jagged edges.

HAIRBRUSHES

New babies are usually somewhat lacking in the hair department, so you might well assume they don't need hairbrushes. However brushes can still be useful, as arguably brushing the scalp with circular strokes daily helps prevent cradle cap (scaly patches that appear on some young babies' scalps) and stimulates hair growth. Regardless, the brush won't be wasted as sooner or later your baby will sprout more hair.

Slightly firmer brushes are more effective on a baby's hair than the very soft ones.

Hairbrush
Kent baby

CHAPTER 4

BREAST- AND BOTTLE-FEEDING EQUIPMENT AND WEANING ITEMS

DECIDING ON HOW TO FEED

There's been a major push in recent years to encourage mums to breastfeed, with a government recommendation that breastfeeding until at least six months is best. We're not going to debate the merits of breast versus formula milk here as there's plenty of information elsewhere on this. Some mums find breastfeeding a doddle, others struggle (although attending breastfeeding classes, reading up on techniques and seeking advice quickly if feeding isn't going well, can make all the difference).

Most of us have a preference about which route we'd like to go down before our baby arrives, but bear in mind that with feeding, even the best-laid plans can change.

In terms of equipment, even if you plan to breastfeed exclusively, you may still need to give the occasional bottle should you decide to return to work, want or need someone to do a feed or if you suffer from mastitis. This means you'll also, as with bottlefeeding mums, require a steriliser as well.

BREASTFEEDING ACCESSORIES

While you can manage with just the 'equipment' nature provides (!), a few products can help to ease things along.

SHOPPING LIST

Breastfeeding
- ✓ Breast pump *(essential if you develop mastitis or engorgement)*
- ✓ Breast pads
- ✓ Nipple cream
- ✓ 3 breastfeeding bras
- ✓ 2 feeding bottles
- ? Breast milk storage containers/bags
- ? Nipple shells/shields
- ✗ Breastfeeding clothes

Bottlefeeding
- ✓ 6 feeding bottles
- ✓ Formula
- ✓ Formula dispenser
- ? Flask

Both breast and bottle
- ✓ Steriliser
- ✓ Bottle brush
- ✓ Burp cloths/muslins and bibs
- ? Feeding pillow
- ? Insulated bottle holder
- ? Dishwasher basket
- ? Bottle drying rack
- ✗ Bottlewarmer

Weaning *(at around six months)*
- ✓ Weaning spoons and bowls
- ✓ Storage tubs and cubes
- ✓ Weaning bibs
- ✓ Highchair
- ✓ Training cups *(from about one year)*
- ? Baby food blender or hand blender *(if making purées for weaning)*

BREAST PUMPS

These allow you to express milk, which can then be given to your baby in a bottle (or dropper for premature babies or those who are too ill to suck). We must warn you that although worthy, having your boobs squeezed by a machine until milk squirts out certainly isn't one of the most glamorous aspects of parenthood. In its simplest form, a manual pump has a funnel-like end that attaches to your breast and a lever or rubber ball that you press to pump your milk into a bottle or container. Electric versions have a motor, which does the hard work for you.

Do you really need one?

It is possible to express by hand but most women prefer to use a pump. One will certainly be handy if any of the following apply.

If you're returning to work, start expressing well in advance to get your baby used to a bottle; some babies take a while to adapt if they've only ever been breastfed.

❉ You're returning to work and want your baby to have breast milk when you're not with her.

❉ You'd like someone else to give your baby a bottle of breast milk occasionally so you can have a break.

❉ Your baby is hospitalised, has a feeding problem or is too ill to feed directly from the breast but you want her to have breast milk (although note that pumps are nearly always available in special-care baby units and some hospitals lend them out for home use in such scenarios).

❉ Your breasts become engorged (too full of milk) or you start developing mastitis (inflammation of the breast); a pump will help ease these conditions.

When do you need it?

We recommend buying a pump before the birth but leaving it unopened and keeping the receipt in case you don't use it or find you'd prefer a different type.

Hiring a pump

You can rent 'hospital grade' breast pumps (try the National Childbirth Trust or www.expressyourselfmums.com) but unless you'll only need it for a very short period, this usually works out more expensive than buying. The better 'consumer' models these days are often as good as hospital grade ones.

THE MAIN BUYING DECISIONS
Manual or electric?

Electric pumps cost more but are usually quicker and less tiring for your hands. If you'll express every day, then they're a must. Indeed, if you're likely to express even a moderate amount, we still think it's worth paying extra for an electric pump. If, however, you have an exceptionally good milk supply or will only express very occasionally, you could make do with a manual (you will only know this post-birth so if the pump you originally bought is no longer right for you, exchange it).

Double or single?

Double pumps allow simultaneous expressing from both breasts, speeding the process up. Singles are generally cheaper and will suffice for most mums, but if you're going to be expressing on a very regular basis, or have twins, a double is worth the investment.

Don't pay extra for...

Integrated pump plus feeding 'systems'. Some manufacturers boast that their pumps 'integrate' with their baby bottles for convenience. However, that particular manufacturer's bottles might not suit your baby (breastfed babies can be very fussy when first bottlefeeding and the teat brand can make a significant difference). Expressing into any sterile container and pouring the milk into a baby bottle isn't so much extra hassle.

BREAST MILK STORAGE

Expressed milk can be stored in sterile containers or bags in the fridge or freezer. Some pumps integrate with specific manufacturers' storage bags or bottles but generally you can use any sterile container or any make of milk storage bag. If you use bags, sit them in a sterile tub to prevent wasting milk in case of leaks.

BREAST PADS

Breast pads sit in your bra, soaking up the milk leaks which are pretty inevitable post-birth (and sometimes in pregnancy) and which can cause soggy patches on clothing. There are

☀ Breast Pump
Single electric: Medela **Swing** (very efficient); **Medela Mini Electric** (noisy but cheaper and adequate for less frequent expressing)

☀ *Double electric:* **Ameda Egnell Lactaline; Medela Freestyle** (both pricey but powerful and very portable)

✳ **Breast Pads**
Disposable: Lansinoh
Disposable Nursing Pads;
Johnson's Baby Nursing
Pads • ✿ Natracare New
Mother Breast Pads

disposable and reusable versions. Disposables are more convenient but less eco-friendly (although you can now buy biodegradable ones). Reusables (either washable fabric or silicone pads) are the more cost-effective and greener choice.

NIPPLE SHIELDS AND PROTECTORS

Shields are small, shaped plastic devices that sit between your nipples and your baby's mouth during feeds. They're not normally necessary unless you have inverted nipples, a baby who is too weak to feed without them or has tongue tie/a palate problem, or you have extremely sore nipples and other remedies you have tried haven't solved the problem.

According to lactation experts, the problem with shields is that they can inhibit breastfeeding if babies get too used to the feel of them and they can start to refuse feeds without them. For this reason, they are best avoided. But, in the situations mentioned above, they can be beneficial. Generally, if you have inverted or flat nipples it's worthwhile purchasing a set in advance, otherwise just be aware of where you can get them if needed at short notice.

Breast shells (also known as protectors), are silicone shell-like covers and less problematic as they aren't worn during feeds but go in your bra to prevent sore nipples chafing against clothing and/or to collect milk if you suffer excessive leakage and breast pads are not enough. A good tip is to add cottonwool to the shells to prevent a mess when you remove them.

Verdict: most women manage without shields and shells/protectors, so only purchase them if and when they're needed.

✳ **Nipple Cream**
Lansinoh Cream for Sore
Nipples (a favourite of
breastfeeding experts),
Motherlove Nipple
Cream (lanolin-free),
Multi-Mam Nipple Balm
(natural and lanolin-free)

NIPPLE CREAMS

These are for mothers rather than babies but essential to soothe sore and cracked nipples.

BREASTFEEDING BRAS

You've probably already bought maternity bras, so you might be wondering why you need to cough up for another set. As with good maternity bras, breastfeeding bras should be supportive and adjustable – the crucial difference is that the

cups undo, usually with hook fastenings, to allow easier access to the breast at feeding time. Moreover, your boobs might have expanded since early pregnancy and could become even more ample post-birth, so breastfeeding bras are stretchy yet supportive, allowing for the size changes that can occur throughout the day and night in the postnatal period.

Do you really need them?
If you intend to breastfeed, then yes, as they make life easier and more comfortable. We recommend buying three (one on, one spare, one in the wash) but keep the packaging and receipts in case you need a different size or breastfeeding doesn't work out.

When do you need to buy them?
Get fitted for breastfeeding bras after 36 weeks of pregnancy – Marks & Spencer, John Lewis and the National Childbirth Trust offer fitting services. Don't get measured earlier as there could still be last-minute changes to your body.

Look for...
* *Wide straps* to add support and prevent cutting into your shoulders.
* *Machine-washable fabrics* since now is not the time for hand-washing lingerie.
* *As much cotton as possible* to help keep your breasts cool if they get engorged.
* *Cups that are easy to undo* and do up again one-handed (you'll be holding your baby).
* *Non-wired bras* as wires can cause breast lumps or mastitis in breastfeeding women.

BREASTFEEDING CLOTHING
Nightwear, tops and dresses specially designed for feeding aren't a necessity; you can just wear normal clothes with easy access to your boobs at feeding time (buttoned nighties or pjs and shirts and wrap tops). Breastfeeding clothing might be worthwhile, however, if you carry your baby in a sling a lot. Otherwise, if you feel the need to guard your modesty, you

✸ Breastfeeding Bras
£ Mothercare (pretty and well-priced) • **££ Noppies** (basic but comfortable), **Bravado** • **£££ Elle MacPherson, Hot Milk** (for those who want something glam)

Nursing Cover
Bebe au Lait

could drape a scarf, poncho or large muslin across yourself, or invest in a purpose-designed feeding cover-up; Bebe au Lait's are excellent as they have a 'hoop' neckline so you can maintain eye contact and see what your baby's doing. They can also help later on, when slightly older, more curious babies can get distracted from feeding by goings-on around them.

BOTTLEFEEDING

BOTTLES AND TEATS

Feeding bottles used to be simple affairs – glass or plastic bottles with latex teats. Then, as with many other baby products, things got much more complicated, with 'anti-colic systems', 'variflow orthodontic teats', designer versions from the likes of Dior, and even a bottle that looks like a breast. Visit, say, Boots or Mothercare these days to buy bottles, and it's easy to end up staring blankly at the huge selection, wondering which to choose. But we're here to get to the bottom of it all starting with some basics.

Baby bottles sold in the UK and EU are no longer allowed to contain a substance called BPA (bisphenol-A), which may disrupt a baby's hormone levels. Be aware, however, that if you buy or borrow older, secondhand bottles, these might not be BPA-free.

How many?

This depends on how you'll feed your baby.

❊ *If solely bottlefeeding,* buy six (tiny babies typically have this many feeds daily so this allows you to only have to sterilise them once a day).

❊ *If mixed feeding (both breast and bottle with either expressed or formula milk),* buy two for now and more if you increase bottlefeeds.

❊ *If breastfeeding only,* buy two bottles for giving expressed milk or just in case things don't work out.

Bottles and Teats
Dr Brown's, BornFree, Tommee Tippee Closer to Nature, Medela Calma (expensive, but good for combining with breastfeeding)

Look for...

❊ *An appropriate teat for your baby's stage* Some bottles include newborn teats, some only faster-flow ones; you can buy different teats separately, if needed.

❊ *Ease of cleaning* Don't under-estimate the importance of this; you'll be scrubbing up to six bottles a day. Some brands have many components, making them harder to wash,

BABY BOTTLE TERMINOLOGY

✳ *Teat* This is the soft bit the baby sucks on (sometimes also known as a nipple). Some are made from clear silicone, others from the more traditional latex (yellowy rubber). Silicone is more durable and easier to clean; latex needs changing frequently as it can deteriorate over time. Latex, however, is natural, softer and more 'skin-like'. Some brands such as Nuk and Bibi offer a choice of latex or silicone teats, whereas the market leaders, Avent and Dr Brown's, only produce silicone ones. You can sometimes use a different brand of teat on a specific bottle but watch out for leaks.

✳ *Flow rate* Teats come in slow, medium, fast and variable flows. The rate and/or number of holes at the top determines how much milk a baby gets when sucking. Slow is usually best for newborns, medium from three to six months and fast from six months plus. If your baby gets frustrated or falls asleep midway through feeds, try a faster-flowing teat. Thicker, 'hungry baby' formula also requires faster-flow teats. Variable flow versions offer several rates in one teat depending on which way up you put the bottle into your baby's mouth.

✳ *Anti-colic system/valve* Some bottles are marketed as being able to reduce the amount of air taken in, preventing windiness and colic, which can make babies unsettled. Manufacturers tout their own research to back these claims but given the lack of independent evidence and the fact no one really knows what causes colic, the jury is still out on this. That said, if you have a colicky baby, you'll probably go with any potential solution so such bottles are worth trying.

assemble and fit in sterilisers. The otherwise excellent Dr Brown's bottles suffer from this. Bear in mind that wide-neck bottles are generally easier to clean (and fill) than narrow-necked ones.

✳ *Dishwasher safety* You need to wash bottles as well as sterilising them, and sometimes you may wish to use a dishwasher. Most bottles are dishwasher safe, provided they go on the top rack; however, frequent dishwashing could reduce a bottle's lifespan by causing scratches.

✳ *Breastfeeding 'compatibility'* If you're planning to offer bottles of breast milk or to mixed feed, choose a bottle that complements breastfeeding (see product showcase (page 59).

Dinky newborn-size bottles (120–150ml) have a limited life; all too soon your baby will be guzzling feeds too big to fit in them. You can use full-size bottles from the start as long as they have newborn teats fitted.

If your baby isn't getting on with a particular bottle, before buying a whole new set, try another brand of teat on your existing bottles.

Glass bottles are an eco-conscious choice. Made without petrochemicals, they can last for years or be recycled when no longer needed. They are, however, heavier to carry around and can break. If you're interested in these, check out Green Baby, Born Free or Lifefactory's Wee Go ranges.

Disposable Bottles
Vital Baby

Steer clear of...

❉ Choosing a bottle brand just because it integrates with a breast pump (see also page 53).

●✦ *When your baby is ready to move on to a cup, bottle 'systems' turn bottles into trainer cups by the addition of toddler spouts and handles. These can be worthwhile, although your baby might not take to that brand's spout (even if he liked the bottles), so just buy one spout and see if your toddler accepts it before buying a full set.*

SPECIALIST BOTTLES AND TEATS

If your baby is premature or has a sucking or palate problem, Medela's Special Needs or Cup Feeders may be recommended. This or other specialist equipment also can be worth trying if you have a breastfed baby who is refusing standard bottles.

DISPOSABLE BOTTLES

Single-use bottles mean no washing and sterilising when travelling. They take up a lot of luggage space on the outward journey and aren't very eco-friendly. Check before packing whether your baby will even accept a disposable bottle's teat if he's used to a different type. We're not keen on Playtex's system with disposable liners as you still have to wash the reusable teats and they can be fiddly to use.

FORMULA

Infant milks are fairly standard, so unless your doctor or health visitor specifies a particular brand, choose one formulated to

PRODUCT SHOWCASE

Medela's Calma bottle and **Solitaire teat** are purpose-designed for combining with breastfeeding: the teat requires a baby to use the same muscles as he does at the breast. Moreover, the teat comes in one size only and milk flow is totally controlled by the baby's strength of sucking. However, it's unlikely to be suitable if you're switching from another brand of bottle, as your baby will probably find it too much effort; the teat is best for little ones who have previously only been breastfed.

Solitaire teats can be bought separately for use on any standard-neck bottle, but they won't fit on the more commonly used wide-neck ones. They're also considerably more expensive than most but as there's only one size, they should last all the way to when your baby stops having bottles. For mums committed to continuing breastfeeding, they could be a wise investment.

your baby's age; you will need to read the label carefully. It is vitally important to prepare the powder as directed.

Ready-to-feed liquid formula is more expensive than powder but can be safer in certain circumstances because it is simply poured into a bottle without any preparation. Current guidelines recommend ready-to-feed formula for sick, premature or otherwise vulnerable babies.

FORMULA DISPENSERS

These handy canisters hold pre-measured powdered formula portions for when you're out. Mothercare, Avent and Tommee Tippee all make them but we've found Brother Max's the most effective at stopping powder spilling from one section to another; they're a little bulkier but come with a handy funnel to decant formula with minimal spillage.

"I keep a few cartons of ready-made formula for when we're out. It's more expensive than powder but also very useful when I don't have any cooled boiled water or have run out of powder."

Formula Dispenser
Brother Max Milk Powder Dispenser

PRODUCT SHOWCASE

Chillipeeps are clever re-usable teats which fix directly onto a carton of ready-made formula. If you bottlefeed, they'd be handy to keep in your changing bag if ever you're without a clean bottle or enough formula milk. They can be washed in a dishwasher and sterilised ready for next time. You can buy either pre-sterilised or standard versions.

Flask
Tommee Tippee Closer to
Nature Travel Bottle
Warmer

FLASK

If you'll need to warm bottles at night or when out, a wide, insulated bottle-warming flask will keep water hot for several hours – simply stand the bottle in the hot water for a few minutes. Flasks are also recommended to hold sterile water for mixing formula when out and about. However, if you get your baby used to room-temperature milk, you won't have to warm his bottles.

INSULATED BOTTLE HOLDERS

Some changing bags come with these included. Otherwise wait and see if you need one.

BOTTLEWARMERS

We would suggest not bothering with these as most take too long! If you must warm milk, it's usually quicker to sit the bottle in a jug of hot water (supplied by a kettle) or use a flask.

DISHWASHER BASKETS

These are cheap and although by no means essential, they keep teats and smaller items from falling off the shelf on to the dishwasher element below where they might melt.

BOTTLE DRYING RACKS

OK, they prevent bottles from tipping over, but what's wrong with a normal dish rack?

STERILISERS

Do you really need one?

Sterilisers are essential for bottlefeeding (with expressed milk or formula) and potentially for bowls and spoons during the first stages of weaning if you introduce solids before six months. UK recommendations are to sterilise all milk-feeding equipment until your baby is a year old, although many parents question how necessary this is once their baby is putting everything, clean or unclean, into his teeny mouth. In our opinion it is worth sticking with the guidelines and sterilising milk bottles throughout the first year, as warm milk provides an ideal breeding ground for bacteria. Yes, our

American friends just use their dishwashers but if you don't have one or don't run it daily, this means washing bottles by hand in between. Sterilising provides extra reassurance that hand-washed bottles are germ free.

You can sterilise equipment in a pan of boiling water for 10 minutes but it's a faff and, for sleep-deprived new parents, it's all too easy to accidentally leave the pan to boil dry, potentially ruining both the pan and its contents. We think it's worth investing in a proper unit – it should get plenty of use.

When do you need it?

If you think you'll bottlefeed early on, purchase a steriliser in advance of the birth. Otherwise you can wait and buy it if you introduce bottles.

Look for...

❖ *A decent capacity* What's needed depends on your feeding method. If you mainly or exclusively bottlefeed, you'll probably prefer to sterilise a full day's worth at once – usually six bottles for a newborn. If you mainly breastfeed, this is less of an issue, but a decent-sized one will still be valuable so you can fit a breast pump and weaning bowls into it.

❖ *Speed* Waiting 12 minutes for the steriliser to finish while your baby screams for a feed because you forgot to switch it on is not a relaxing experience. The fastest steam sterilisers take five minutes, microwave ones take from two to eight minutes. Quicker is obviously better.

Steer clear of...

❖ Buying a steriliser because it includes some free bottles with it; the bottles might not be the best choice for your baby.

TYPES OF STERILISER
Cold water

This involves placing a chemical sterilising tablet or liquid into a large container of water and soaking the feeding equipment in it for at least 15 to 30 minutes, depending on the brand.

+ Cheap.

+ Very portable; you can use any plastic tub.

− Some parents don't like the idea of using a chemical solution on feeding equipment and some babies dislike the residual taste (though you can rinse the bottles in cooled, boiled water).

− Need to remember to keep a stock of tablets or solution and to change the solution every 24 hours.

− More time consuming and messy than other options.

Verdict: Only worth considering if you have items that can only be cold-water sterilised (this is rare) or if you are travelling and don't have access to a microwave or electric travel steriliser.

Microwave

Microwave sterilisers are more compact than electric alternatives, although you must check the steriliser will fit in your microwave before buying and whether your oven has to be a turntable model. These are simply glorified lidded plastic boxes. You place your feeding equipment and a measured amount of water into the box and put it in the microwave for two to eight minutes, depending on the steriliser and your microwave's wattage.

This last point is key: certain manufacturers boast of sterilisation times of as little as two minutes, but if you look carefully, this is for a super-powerful 1100-watt microwave; most newish domestic models are only around 700 to 900 watts, which would take four minutes (still reasonably quick though).

❋ Microwave Steriliser
Philips Avent, Tommee Tippee, Dr Brown's

Many microwave sterilisers have a smaller capacity (normally four bottles although a few, including Avent's, take six), so If you bottlefeed exclusively, a smaller steriliser won't allow you to do all the day's bottles at once, which could be annoying. Moreover, some breast pumps and metal cutlery cannot be sterilised in a microwave.

Microwave sterilisers are light to carry when travelling (see also page 63) and although they're bulky, you can store bottles in them to make the best use of space.

+ Cheaper than electric sterilisers.
+ Normally quite quick.
+ Easy to take on holiday.
+ Take up less work surface space than an electric steriliser.
‑ May have a smaller capacity (4 rather than 6 bottles).
‑ You need a big enough microwave to take the box.
‑ Can't sterilise anything metallic.

Electric steam

This is an effective choice if you plan to solely or mainly bottlefeed or have twins and will need to sterilise a lot of bottles daily. They have a kettle-style element, which boils a small amount of water turning it into steam, which kills bacteria.

It's important to choose a model that's quick (the best take five to six minutes). Some newer steam sterilisers allow a continuous cycle to run, keeping contents sterile for 24 hours but this isn't necessary; we've never heard of a baby being harmed by unused bottles that were sterilised a few hours beforehand.

On the downside, electric sterilisers are bulky and will need de-scaling periodically if you live in a hard-water area, but if you'll bottlefeed a lot or don't own a microwave (or a decent-sized one), their convenience makes up for this.

+ Usually very efficient.
+ Larger capacity than most microwave sterilisers.
‑ Take up work surface space.
‑ More expensive.
‑ Need de-scaling if you live in a hard-water area.

Verdict: Go for a large-capacity microwave steriliser if your oven is big enough and powerful enough to sterilise quickly. Otherwise choose an electric steam model with a quick cycle.

Electric Steriliser
Philips Avent

Travel sterilisers

If you'll have access to a microwave when you're away, microwavable steriliser bags are very convenient. You simply put one or two washed bottles into a purpose-designed bag, pour in a little water and put the bag in the microwave for

Travel Steriliser
Babytec electric; Lindam
or Medela microwave
bags

three minutes. The bags pack away to virtually nothing and can be reused up to 20 times but since they only take two bottles at a time, they aren't suitable for daily use.

Another portable option is Babytec's electric travel steam steriliser. It only takes two bottles at a time but is easy to use and we recommend it for travelling if no microwave is available. If you are staying somewhere very basic, with no electricity or microwave, or camping, a plastic tub and some Milton steriliser tablets will do the job.

Bottle Brush
Perfectly Happy People/
PHP Baby Bottle Scrubber
and Teat Scrubber; Dr
Brown's Bottle and Teat
Brush

BOTTLE CLEANING BRUSHES

Bottles and other feeding equipment must be washed before sterilising, and a bottle brush will help ensure thorough cleaning. Sponge-tipped, rather than bristle, brushes are the best for cleaning without scratching and reaching all the edges with ease.

FEEDING PILLOWS

These sound like a luxury but by improving positioning, they can contribute significantly to breastfeeding's success. If you're expecting twins and wish to breastfeed both simultaneously, they're essential.

Bottlefeeders will also find such pillows a useful way to get comfortable, position their baby and prevent poor posture while feeding. Some feeding pillows can double as an aid to comfortable sleeping in pregnancy and later on as a support when your baby is learning to sit.

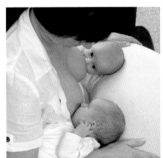

Look for...

❋ *A washable, removable cover.*

MUSLINS/BURP CLOTHS AND BABY BIBS

Feeding small babies can involve some mess. You'll probably find you have a muslin cloth semi-permanently draped over your shoulder in the early days to protect your clothes from baby sick – these thin cloths really are a baby essential. Some shops sell coloured and patterned versions, which can be useful if you want to identify your baby's vomit-covered cloth from someone else's at a mother-and-baby group.

As well as standard-sized muslins (around the same dimensions as a tea towel), you can also buy extra-large ones, such as those made by the American company, aden + anais. These cloths can be thrown over your shoulder in the usual way but are also handy for swaddling, as breastfeeding cover-ups, for draping over prams to block out the sun or as makeshift blankets.

As an alternative to muslins, burp cloths are smaller pieces of fabric, usually made from towelling or cotton jersey and designed to go over your shoulder during winding, again to stop baby vomit getting on your clothing. They're usually nice and soft against your baby's skin, but they can work out more expensive and aren't as versatile so we'd suggest just sticking with muslins.

Soft towelling or cotton baby bibs will adequately soak up milk spills and dribble.

⁂ **Feeding Pillow**
My Brest Friend (single or twin version), Harmony Duo

⁂ **Burp Cloths/ Muslins**
Faye and Lou brightly coloured muslin squares, aden + anais large muslin cloths (a little more expensive but very useful and a lovely new baby gift)

- -

PRODUCT SHOWCASE

We're big fans of the **My Brest Friend Breastfeeding Pillow** (despite the naff name). Unlike standard feeding cushions, it straps around you and has a flat top allowing your baby to lie comfortably without rolling down. It provides good lumbar support, won't slip and leaves your hands free to position your baby or hold a feeding bottle more easily if using one. There's also the larger **Twin Plus** version for twins.

- -

WEANING EQUIPMENT AND TRAINING CUPS

Introducing solid foods is a small but exciting step on your baby's path towards growing up. When to first offer solids is a surprisingly contentious issue. Current UK recommendations are to wait until your baby is six months old, but many parents struggle to hold off this long when faced with a hungry baby showing a keen interest in devouring something other than milk. If you are in this situation, it's wise to discuss early weaning with your health visitor or GP.

When do you need it?

Even if you introduce solids a little earlier than the official guideline of six months, it's unlikely you'll need weaning gear before around five months.

What do you need?

There are two different approaches to weaning and which you take will affect what you need to buy.

The most common way to wean is to spoon feed puréed, easily digestible fruits and vegetables to your baby once you have passed the introductory baby rice stage. Then, gradually, you will introduce more flavours and firmer textures and maybe some 'finger foods'. Our advice on what to buy assumes this approach, as it's what the majority of parents do.

However, an alternative way to introduce solids, 'baby-led weaning' (BLW), has become more popular in recent years. Instead of purées, you put chunks of 'normal' food in front of your baby and let him grab and explore whatever appeals. If you go down this route, you simply pop the food straight on to a highchair tray or the dinner table (maybe with a mat underneath). You might need to buy a couple of plastic bowls and spoons as, at some stage, you'll still need to introduce softer/more liquid foods, such as porridge or cereal. You also probably will find extra bibs handy (see page 68), as BLW can get decidedly messy, but you won't require a blender or baby food storage pots.

SPOONS

The feel of a spoon in your young baby's mouth can be quite alien to him and the type used when weaning can make a difference to how well he accepts solids initially. Soft-tipped plastic spoons are better than harder ones for the early days.

You can manage with two or three, but more means you won't have to wash up every mealtime. Later on, you can introduce firmer plastic or metal spoons.

Spoons
Initially: Vital Baby soft-tipped weaning spoons • *Later on:* Tommee Tippee spoon multipacks

STORAGE TUBS AND CUBES

These are valuable for keeping homemade baby food in the fridge or freezer, or for taking it out with you. Many parents batch cook purées, freeze them and defrost small amounts as needed. Of course, you can use any pots but small baby food ones reduce waste as you only need to defrost the appropriate portion each time. Make sure any that you buy for taking out with you can be sealed securely.

Ice-cube trays are also good for freezing purées. Look for soft silicone ones to make it easier to pop out the portions or individual cubes with lids ('weaning cubes'). Brother Max Food Portioners are especially good – the individual cubes click together and snap apart easily and can be put in the microwave; it's also very easy to pop frozen food out of them.

Storage Tubs
Brother Max Food Portioners

Happy Mummy Baby Cubes, Beaba Multi-Portions Silicone tubs

PLATES AND BOWLS

Babies throw things on the floor, sometimes on purpose, sometimes by accident. You needn't choose specific baby/toddler dishes with kiddy characters but something unbreakable is wise. Some baby/toddler plates and bowls have suckers on the bottom, designed to prevent little diners throwing their bowl (and its contents) on the floor. These can help stop a small child from accidentally elbowing his meal off the table or highchair tray, but they do little to prevent the most determined dinner-chuckers from doing so as the attachment is rarely strong enough.

Bowls are better than plates for older babies who are self-feeding, as they can scoop things up more easily against the high sides. Look for items that can go in the microwave, freezer and dishwasher for convenience.

Plates and Bowls
Baby Björn First Bowl and Spoon set; Ikea's bargain cheap, brightly coloured kids range; Brother Max; TUMTUM; OXO Tot Feeding Set

●→ *For toddler snacks, little pots with flexible, sectioned lids keep the contents inside even if the pot is turned upside-down but allow small fingers to reach in and grab the food. Snack Trap ones attach to a pushchair, car seat or highchair with a tether (sold separately) to make them even more accident proof.*

WEANING BIBS

Weaning Bibs
Bibetta (comfortable, practical neoprene); **Brother Max Catch and Fold** (great for out and about); **Tommee Tippee Roll n Go** (easy to wipe-clean)

There are times when you'll wish so-called solids were actually more solid – baby food can get everywhere and you'll need something more robust than tiny, soft towelling or cotton bibs to help prevent changes of clothing due to errant carrot purée.

Either chose something wipeable with a food-catching pocket at the bottom (sometimes called pelican bibs) or for maximum protection, long-sleeved bibs. The latter also work well for messy toddler activities like finger painting. Buy three or four – they're a little more expensive than standard bibs but one size should last from weaning through to around age two.

BABY FOOD BLENDERS AND PROCESSORS

Food Processor
Beaba Babycook Steamer and Blender

If you'll make purées yourself you'll need to whizz food up into mush. The most cost-effective and easy way to do this is probably with a normal handheld 'stick' blender; even if you buy this specially, you should be able to find a use for it long beyond weaning.

Another option to create purées is a purpose-designed baby food processor, the main one on the market being the Beaba Babycook. Some parents (including one of us!) think highly of this little gadget, which steams, blends, defrosts and reheats baby food in one machine. It saves on washing up, and helps

avoid worries about burns from hotspots in microwaved food. If you're planning on making homemade purées this could be a worthwhile purchase but it is expensive at around £90 and will only be useful for a shortish period. It certainly isn't a 'must-have' and a hand blender is a cheaper alternative, which works well for adult recipes and baby purées alike.

You can also buy small, handheld, non-electric baby food mashers, such as The Wean Machine. These are, in effect, over-sized garlic crushers with an integral bowl and spoon. Although inexpensive and possibly useful when out, they can be tricky to clean, and most don't cope very well with larger quantities or relatively firm food.

RECIPE AND WEANING BOOKS

If you'll make your own baby food, a baby recipe book might provide inspiration although, of course, advice and recipes are available for free on the internet.

TRAINING CUPS

By around the age of one, it's recommended your baby stops using baby bottles and moves on to 'training' or 'spouty' cups. In reality, many babies struggle to adapt to these, so don't worry if yours is a little older when he gives up his bottle. You might have to try several brands to identify one your baby likes, so only buy one initially. When you've worked out which suits your baby, you'll need two or three more.

HIGHCHAIRS

From weaning until your baby is big and sensible enough to sit in a grown-up chair, a highchair will be a major feature of your kitchen. Choose the style wisely and you needn't wince at some garish monstrosity on a daily basis. However, whether you go for cheap and cheerful or swanky and pricey, it's crucial that it's easy to clean as it will regularly get covered in gunk.

Do you really need one?

You do need some sort of chair in which to feed your baby, although it doesn't have to be a conventional highchair (see below).

✳ Books
Baby-Led Weaning by Gill Rapley and Tracey Murkett (Vermilion, 2008) *Weaning and First Foods* by Nicola Graimes (Carroll & Brown, 2009);

✳ Training Cup
Tommee Tippee First Cup

✳ **Portable Highchair**
£ Argos • **££** The First
Years, Safety 1st Tray
Feeding Booster • **££/£££**
Beaba Babyboost (more
stylish); Phil&Teds Me Too
or Lobster seats (clamp
straight on to the kitchen
or dining table), Handysitt

When do you need it?

Ideally, when your baby is able to sit without support as otherwise you will have to surround him with padding. When you start weaning, you could use a bouncy chair or 'Bumbo' type seat, delaying purchasing a highchair until your baby reaches six to nine months of age.

THE MAIN BUYING DECISIONS
'Proper' highchair or portable seat?

The majority of parents purchase a full-size/proper highchair but you can save money by starting off with a bouncy chair and then buying a cheaper portable highchair once your baby can sit up at the table without support. A portable highchair takes up less space and can be used away from home. Those we recommend are particularly good for full-time use at home.

Wood or metal?

Wooden highchairs have staged a comeback in recent years as more attractive alternatives to plastic and metal versions. Metal highchair manufacturers have, in turn, upped the style ante with funkier designs that are more pleasing to the eye. Wooden models tend to have fewer nooks and crannies for food to lodge in so are easier to clean. Some wooden highchairs convert into adult chairs later on (for example, the Stokke Tripp Trapp). Metal models generally are more comfortable and supportive for younger babies, and can be lighter and easier to move around.

Tray or no tray?

Highchairs can have a fixed or removable tray or no tray at all. Models lacking trays are placed up against the kitchen/dining table, the idea being that your baby learns about eating and table manners earlier because he'll be more 'integrated' into family meals. We buy into this philosophy and believe it works, but if you prefer to contain mess (as far as you can) or have a particularly precious dining table, a tray might be wise.

A highchair with a removable tray allows you to start off with the tray when your baby is young and to remove it at the toddler stage when he may sit at the table.

PRODUCT SHOWCASE

Bumbo and **Prince Lionheart BebePod** These rubber/plastic tub chairs support a baby at the stage where he'd quite like to sit up but can't manage it alone. They're touted as useful for early weaning but since they have to be used on the floor (they must never be placed on raised surfaces), they aren't that comfortable for the 'feeder' who has to crouch alongside. Our parent panel is divided on these; some parents regard them as 'wastes of money' but a few loved theirs. Worryingly, some parents report that their baby could flip themselves out of their Bumbo, although to be fair, the manufacturers openly state that the seat is not meant to be restrictive and a baby shouldn't use it unattended.

Of the two, the BebePod is harder plastic and some of its variations feature a safety belt to stop a baby flipping out of it. Both the Bumbo and BebePod have optional trays.

The window of use for these products is very short, so we think these aren't a worthwhile purchase but if you really want one, buy second-hand or borrow, and never use one on an elevated surface.

Do you want it to last beyond the baby stage?
Some highchairs are more adjustable than others and are roomy enough for older toddlers. Some (usually wooden ones) convert to adult chairs later on. Overall, convertible highchairs tend to be pricier and are only worthwhile if you actually like the style of the chair they become (although our recommended options are excellent highchairs anyway).

Does it need to fold?
If space is tight in your kitchen, consider a highchair that folds up when not in use. Metal models usually do, although check the folded dimensions as some collapse down more compactly than others. Basic highchairs are often better for this than 'all-singing' ones; the Stokke Tripp Trapp is particularly slim even though it doesn't fold. Another option if there's limited space, is to go with a bouncy chair followed by a portable highchair.

Look for...
Essential
❊ *Easy cleaning* Avoid anything with lots of nooks and crannies In which food can lodge. Look for smooth surfaces that will

⁂ **Highchair**
£ **Ikea Antilop** (metal/plastic with tray option) •
£££ **Stokke Tripp Trapp** (wooden and converts to an adult chair), **OXO Tot Sprout**

⁂ ££ **Graco Contempo** (metal/plastic, lots of features); **Cosatto On The Move** (metal/plastic, folds down especially well so ideal for compact kitchens); **Chicco Jazzy** (attractive, inexpensive and easy to clean); **Baby-Dan Danchair** (wooden, similar to Stokke Tripp Trapp but cheaper) • £££ **Brother Max Scoop and Bloom Fresco Loft** (both super-cool, no nooks and crannies but super-expensive, too)

be easy to wipe down. If it has a cushion, check that this is washable or wipeable.

⁂ *Adjustability* The highchair should suit your baby from early weaning through to when he's ready to sit on a regular chair (about five to six months up to two or three years of age).

⁂ *Easy access* You need to be able to get your baby in and out of the highchair easily. Check whether the tray (if there is one) will get in the way or can be moved aside, pulled outwards or lifted off with ease.

⁂ *A supportive seat* In the early stages of weaning, you'll need the highchair to be supportive so your baby feels comfortable and secure. Some models have a cushion (included or at extra cost) to help with this. It's crucial that the cushion is washable or wipeable.

⁂ *A 'crotch' bar* This sits between your baby's legs to prevent him slipping down. If there's no bar, you will definitely need to use a harness (see below). If a highchair has a bar, some parents feel it's sufficiently safe not to use a harness as, in any event, a baby in a highchair should always be supervised. We aren't big fans of harnesses, so favour highchairs with crotch bars.

⁂ *An integral harness or D-rings for a harness attachment* You will definitely need a harness if there is no crotch bar. Although we prefer avoiding harnesses (they're fiddly to open, a nightmare if a baby is choking and difficult to clean), if you end up with a particularly adventurous toddler who tries to climb out of his highchair, you'll have no choice but to add one to prevent accidents.

⁂ *A design that you can live with* Your highchair is going to sit in your kitchen for at least the next couple of years so you need to like it; don't, however, just be seduced by style alone.

Useful

⁂ *Castors* Some highchairs are quite heavy so castors will be helpful if you will move yours around a lot, say, between a kitchen and dining room.

PRODUCT SHOWCASE

Ikea's Antilop Highchair is inoffensive looking, extremely easy to clean, very portable (you can quickly remove the legs and put them plus the seat in the car to take to the grandparents'), and cheap. At under £15 this is one of the best baby bargains around (it's less than a fiver extra for the optional tray). It's also especially good for twins; two 'normal' highchairs cost a fortune and take up a lot of space whereas Antilops can be stacked on top of each other.

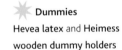

If your baby has a dummy, buy a 'soother saver' to clip it to his clothes, preventing it from falling on the floor and getting grubby.

Don't pay extra for...

✳ *A recline feature* You really don't need this unless you have a pet and, instead of a bouncy chair, would prefer a seat that keeps your pre-weaning baby off the floor during nap times downstairs.

✳ *Integral toy tidies* Unnecessary and another place for food thrown/dropped off the highchair to gather.

DUMMIES

Not strictly feeding gear, but as well as being a sleeping aid and comforter, dummies can be a useful alternative to the breast for 'sucky' babies in between feeds. They're controversial little things, with countless debates about their pros and cons. It's an entirely personal decision as to whether you want your baby to have one or not.

Dummies
Hevea latex and Heimess wooden dummy holders

If you do, orthodontic soothers are preferable to round/cherry-shaped ones as they're less likely to damage a baby's teeth and jaw formation, although some parents find the cherry ones stay better in their baby's mouth. Clear silicone teats last longer than latex but latex feels more skin-like, so might be acceptable to babies who've rejected silicone. Latex is also a natural material.

If your baby develops a preference for a particular type of dummy, buy spares as they tend to get lost.

CHAPTER 5

BABY BEDS
AND BEDDING

SLEEP MATTERS

If the most precious thing in new parents' lives is their baby,
you can bet the second most precious thing will be sleep.

SHOPPING LIST

? Small first bed such as a Moses basket, crib or
carrycot, plus mattress, or hammock

✓ Cot or cot-bed, plus mattress

✓ Bedding *(if using a smaller first bed you will need two
sets in different sizes)*: 3–4 fitted and flat sheets, 2
mattress protectors and 4 blankets unless using sleep
bags (2–3) in which case you need less blankets and
no flat sheets

? Moses basket/carrycot stand

? Baby sheepskin

? Swaddling wrap

? Cot bumpers

? Cot separator *(for twins only)*

? Cat net *(essential if you have a cat)*

✗ Sleep positioners

✗ Quilts, coverlets and pillows *(not under 12 months)*

Among new parents it's sure to be a hot topic of conversation. The short-term goal is to attain the Holy Grail of 'sleeping through the night'. Of course, how long it's going to be before you get a vaguely decent night's sleep won't be determined solely by where your baby sleeps or what she sleeps in, but such things can make life a little easier during this most exhausting of times.

The early days (and nights)

Guidelines from the Foundation for the Study of Infant Deaths (FSID) say the safest place for a baby to sleep at night during her first six months is in your bedroom (but not in your bed). Bedroom sharing also makes night-time feeds slightly more bearable, with no stumbling across a chilly, dark hallway at three in the morning.

Be warned, though, that while newborns are small, they can be disproportionately noisy sleepers and this may affect how long it takes before you pack your little one off to her own room; for some, it feels right to room share for years; for others, it's a relief to no longer hear every snore, groan or moan their baby makes.

New babies sleep a lot (frustratingly not always when you want them to) so think about where yours will nap in the day, and whether you want a portable first bed so you can keep a close eye on her, or are happy to be in different rooms, perhaps using a baby monitor for reassurance.

SLEEPING CHOICES

Many parents choose a smaller first sleeping place for their newborn, usually a Moses basket, carrycot or crib, before moving their baby into a proper cot. Not yet mainstream, but growing in popularity, are baby hammocks. While it's perfectly safe for your newborn to sleep in a full-size cot from day one, tiny babies look, and possibly feel, rather lost in these. After being tightly cosseted in Mum's tum, sleeping in a cot must be the equivalent of an adult bedding down for the night on the pitch at Wembley Stadium – not exactly cosy.

Crucially, if your baby starts off sleeping in your bedroom (as recommended), a smaller first bed takes up considerably less

floor space than a standard cot and, if you choose a portable option (a carrycot or Moses basket), you can cart your slumbering newborn around the house with you.

When budgeting, consider that these smaller beds will be outgrown quickly; within three or four months and certainly by six months, most babies need a proper cot. Note, too, that it's not just the Moses basket, crib or carrycot itself you need to pay for, but also an extra set of smaller bedding – sheets, mattress protectors and potentially blankets (if you don't use sleeping bags). So the cheapest option is to use a cot or cot-bed from birth.

A bedside cot or crib (see page 85) is especially good for a newborn as it can be pushed flush to your bed with no barrier between you and your baby, making night feeds easier and aiding bonding. However, these cots or cribs can't be moved around easily, so if you prefer to keep your baby nearby at all times, you'll need another bed in which she can nap.

If you buy and/or borrow wisely or have a generous budget, you could have more than one first sleeping place such as a cot or crib upstairs and a carrycot, Moses basket or hammock downstairs. This could help your baby differentiate between day and night earlier (which aids sleeping through the night).

MAKING THE RIGHT CHOICE

In order to work out whether you need an additional bed to a cot, think carefully about the following:

❊ Do you want to keep your newborn close during daytime naps as well as at night? If so, choose a Moses basket or carrycot rather than a crib or cot.

❊ Is space very limited in your bedroom (assuming your baby will sleep in there at first)? If so, one of the smaller first beds will be particularly valuable.

❊ How much can you afford/do you want to spend on something that will only be used for a few months? While Moses baskets are usually cheaper than cribs and carrycots, the cheapest option is to use a cot from the start.

❊ Do you plan to have more children so perhaps feel that you'll get more value out of a smaller first bed, as it can be used for subsequent babies?

BED CHOICES

	Moses basket	Crib	Carrycot	Hammock	Cot or cot-bed from birth
Typical cost	£40–£100 incl. mattress	£50–£150+ plus mattress (£10–£45)	£100–£170 incl mattress	£40–£150+ incl. mattress	£50–£400+ plus mattress (£35–£300)
Extra bedding?	Yes	Yes	Yes	Yes	No
Easy to reach from your bed	Only with a stand (around £20)	Yes	Only with a stand (around £20)	Depends on model	Only if there is a drop side
Portability	Good	Poor	Good	Depends	Poor
Rocking motion or movement	Only with a rocking stand	Depends on model	Only with a rocking stand	Yes	No
Lasts until	3 to 4 months	4 to 6 months	4 to 6 months	6 to 9 months depending on model	2½ to 3 years (longer for cot-beds)
Other pros			Multi-purpose: can be used on a pushchair		Not an extra expense as you'll need one eventually
Other cons			Not all are suitable for overnight sleeping	Possible dependence on motion to get to sleep; can make transition to normal cot harder	Takes up the most floor space and some newborns feel lost in a full-size cot

When do you need a bed?

As soon as your baby gets home from hospital. While many cots/cot-beds are available almost immediately, some take up to 12 weeks from ordering to delivery. If you'll use a Moses basket, carrycot or crib from birth, your baby won't need the cot until she is three or four months old, or more, but it's worth doing your research pre-baby if possible.

MOSES BASKETS

For some parents, these little woven baskets, dressed up with valances and canopies, fulfil a sentimental vision of a newborn's bed. Looking solely at practicalities though, their value is less clear-cut. Yes, they're compact and portable, although some people find them awkward to carry. They can be taken to a friend's or relative's house but you might want to buy a travel cot anyway so could use that instead. Also, some babies, inexplicably, hate them.

The biggest criticism of Moses baskets is that they're so small they're usually outgrown by three months, although obviously if you have subsequent children, you will get more use out of one. Certainly if the pram you want comes with a detachable carrycot, you can avoid buying a Moses basket as fundamentally, it does the same job.

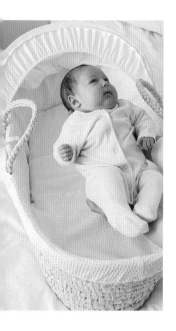

Verdict: Good for the first few weeks as long as you don't spend a fortune; you could borrow one and buy a new mattress.

Look for...
Essential

❄ *A removable, washable lining that isn't too padded* The FSID's advice is that it should be thin to reduce the risk of overheating.

❄ *A sturdy basket that is comfortable to hold* and has secure handles.

❄ *A firm mattress* (mattresses are nearly always included.)

Useful

❄ *A stand* A stand can keep a basket at a convenient height

Moba – a modern Moses basket. Moses baskets don't seem to have changed much since Bible days so perhaps it was about time someone modernised them. Step in Moba, with their strikingly colourful funked up versions. The same shape as a traditional Moses basket but crafted from breathable, easy-to-clean materials, it combines practicality with style and should last several babies.

next to your bed. Some parents place the basket into their baby's cot if they have room for the cot in their bedroom or are putting their baby to bed in her own room from birth. If you buy a stand and it rocks, make sure it can be fixed in position (not all babies love being rocked to sleep).

CRIBS

When it comes to baby kit, Brits and Americans speak different languages. In the US, cribs are what we Brits call cots, whereas over here a crib is what Americans call a cradle – a 'mini' cot suitable for a newborn's first few months. (So if you're an American buying in the UK, make sure you ask for a cot or you'll end up with a small bed that will only last six months.)

Generally made of more substantial material like wood, some cribs may be suspended so they swing, while others have shaped, 'rocking' feet like the base of a rocking chair. Motion sends most babies to sleep but if your crib rocks or swings, check that it can also be locked into a fixed position in case your baby dislikes it. Bear in mind that once your baby moves to a cot, you won't be able to rock her, so if she's used to being rocked to sleep, you might be storing up trouble for later.

A crib is of a similar height to your bed and if it has side bars, you can check on your baby without having to lean over the side – helpful for mums with stitches from a caesarean, tear or episiotomy. However, cribs aren't portable, so if you want your baby nearby during the day, you may need another bed for naps (particularly if your home is on more than one level; if you live in a flat or bungalow, then a crib on castors could be wheeled between rooms).

Mattresses aren't usually included with cribs so will be an added cost. You need to buy one that fits snugly for safety. If your budget allows, a crib for night time and a pram carrycot for daytime naps works well (see combinations below).

As cribs are that bit bigger, they have a slightly longer useful life than Moses baskets – manufacturers and retailers usually say up to six months. You'll need a cot anyway, albeit a month or two later than with a Moses basket or carrycot.

If a traditional, 'fairytale' look is your thing, drapes and canopies can be added to cribs. Your baby will be too young to care how flouncy her crib is, so these are purely decorative and really for your benefit not hers. If co-sleeping with your baby appeals but you are worried about the risks, bedside cribs are worth considering (see page 85).

Look for...
 ❖ *A crib that can be locked in position* if it rocks.

CARRYCOTS
If you're buying a pushchair with a removable carrycot (see page 112), you can skip the Moses basket or crib and use this instead. Some parents prefer the more contemporary look of carrycots to the frillier style of most Moses baskets anyway and they're usually more robust, too.

The biggest advantage of a carrycot though is multi-functionality – you'll get plenty of use out of it – and if your newborn falls asleep in the pram while you're out walking (many reliably doze off with a combination of fresh air and movement), you can unclamp the carrycot and bring it into your living quarters.

Carrycots can be moved from room to room easily and used for overnight sleeping provided the mattress is appropriate; some are too soft or may not be sufficiently 'breathable' for a full night's use. Check with the retailer and, if necessary, buy an extra mattress for night time – foam carrycot mattresses cost between £10 and £20 (see page 88).

The lifespan of a carrycot will be from birth to around six months for use on the pram but by four or five months, it might be too cramped for overnight sleeping.

At night, you can keep the carrycot at a similar height to your bed using a Moses basket stand but because carrycots are bigger, it can be difficult to find a stand that fits (the Mamas & Papas rocking stand works for most carrycots). Manufacturers are realising this can be a problem and a few (Silver Cross's Sleepover, Mamas & Papas' Mylo and Uppababy's Vista) now offer an optional carrycot stand.

Look for...

* *A removable, washable lining* that isn't too padded. The FSID's advice is that it should be thin to reduce the risk of overheating.
* *Comfortable to hold* with secure handles and not too heavy for you to carry round with your baby inside.
* *A firm mattress suitable for overnight sleeping* (if the one included isn't suitable, an extra mattress won't cost much).
* *A carrycot that detaches easily* from the pram – especially for when your baby is asleep in it as you won't wake her.

Verdict: Overall, carrycots can be expensive and if you aren't buying one for your pram, a Moses basket certainly will be cheaper. If you are buying a carrycot for your pram, they're much of a muchness, so focus on the pram's features rather than the carrycot's. Some carrycots are 'car-compatible'; however, with one or two exceptions, we don't recommend their use in cars due to safety concerns (see page 138).

HAMMOCKS

A small but growing number of parents are opting for a baby hammock as their newborn's first bed. The fundamental idea here is that baby hammocks lull babies to sleep by providing multi-directional movement similar to that in the womb. They're also designed to be gently supportive of a baby's spine.

We've heard of many babies who sleep like a dream in hammocks, but not all take to them (although not all babies like cots/Moses baskets either). Fear not if you do buy one and your baby hates it; there's strong secondhand demand so you should recover some, even most, of your money on eBay.

Consider though that when your baby moves to a proper cot or cot-bed, you could be in for a rough time if she's used to the hammock's movement to rock her to sleep. Also, some hammocks are marketed as being suitable sleeping places up to 12 months but we've found most parents stop using theirs once their baby can sit up and move around (by six to nine months). Even if they do last longer than a Moses basket or crib, this won't save you money as you'll need a cot anyway – just a bit later.

There are three main types. The Leander Cradle is a one-off and is covered in the product showcase, below; the other two are conventional and cocoon-style.

Conventional These hammocks are suspended at both ends from a stand – like miniature versions of those garden hammocks you can buy in the likes of Homebase and B&Q.

Cocoon-style These have fabric, which comes up high and a little mattress and are suspended via a single hook from a doorframe or stand. The two best-known models are the Amby Nature's Nest and Moffii Cradle.

Verdict: Overall, hammocks are best viewed as an alternative to a Moses basket, carrycot or crib – not as a longer-term replacement for a cot. Some people think they were key to their newborn's great sleeping habits, others wish they had bought something more conventional. Take some of the manufacturers' claims with a pinch of salt, and decide what appeals to you.

Hammock
Amby Nature's Nest

PRODUCT SHOWCASE

The Leander Cradle This is a Danish product that looks a little like a suspended carrycot and is attached via a single hook to either the ceiling (you'll have to ensure yours is strong enough) or a wooden tripod stand. It's very expensive but quite beautiful!

FULL-SIZE COT OR COT-BED

Whether your baby sleeps in it from birth or uses a smaller 'bed' initially, sooner or later you're going to need a cot or cot-bed. Most babies spend more time in their cot than anywhere else, and the cot contributes significantly to the look of the nursery, so it's worth investing a bit of time in making your choice, in terms of both features and appearance.

Start by deciding whether you want a drop-side model or prefer a cot-bed to a cot. Then look at whether you want a cot/cot-bed that comes as part of a matching range of nursery furniture. There's little point in finding a range you love, and then realising that it only has a cot, not a cot-bed, or fixed rather than drop sides.

To the uninitiated, cots and cot-beds look broadly the same, so what's the difference?

❊ Cot-beds have slightly larger internal dimensions than cots – typically 140 x 70cm compared to 120 x 60cm for a standard cot.

❊ By removing its sides, the cot-bed converts into a 'junior' bed later on. This might last your child until the age of five or six, whereas a cot is normally outgrown (or escaped from – a common trigger for moving a toddler into a bed) around two-and-a-half years of age. Cot-beds make a familiar stepping-stone between a cot and a single bed.

❊ Generally, cot-beds cost more than cots. Don't be fooled into thinking a cot-bed will save you money as you'll still have to buy a single bed for your child just a little later on.

Verdict: The decision probably boils down to how much space you have and cost. If space isn't an issue, a cot-bed is generally better than a cot as it eases the transition to a proper bed.

Look for...
Essential

❊ *At least two different mattress heights* Most models have two or three base positions. You need two – high for a newborn so that it's easier to put her in and take her out, and low for when she can sit up; the lower base position prevents babies flinging themselves over the side. Further

SAFETY TIP

Cots and cot-beds should conform to the safety standard BS-EN 716-1. The bars must be no more than 45mm apart and the mattress should have a low base position. New cots from reputable stores will comply with regulations but secondhand ones and family hand-me-downs might not. The gap between the mattress and cot sides should be less than 40mm. Too tight a fit will make changing bedding difficult so a small gap is best.

positions aren't necessary and changing the base height is an extra job you probably won't want to do too often.

❊ *A durable material* Solid wood will last longer (especially relevant if you want to use the same cot/cot-bed for any subsequent babies); poorer-quality veneer can chip, especially with a toddler regularly bashing toys against it.

Useful

❊ *A drop side* with a quiet mechanism that's operable one-handed. This means one or both cot sides can be lowered, making it easier to get your baby in and out. This isn't an issue for newborns (at that stage you can keep the mattress base high up so you don't have to bend over the cot side). However, once the mattress is lowered to stop older babies climbing out, a drop side is better for your back and a sensible option if you're prone to backache or are short, as bending over the cot side can be a strain. A drop side also allows you to put an already sleeping baby in bed more gently, with less likelihood of her waking. Some work with catches, others with foot pedals; test them out. If the mechanism is noisy, it might jolt your sleeping baby awake.

A NOTE ABOUT DROP SIDES

Cots and cot-beds with drop sides have recently been banned from sale in the US after a number of reported deaths. There are currently no plans to ban them in the EU, where such cots are subject to different and more rigorous safety standards.

We consulted the UK's Baby Products Association on the matter. They said "Drop-sided cots have been used for many decades and there have been no recorded incidents in Europe that would question their safety. As long as parents purchase products from reputable retailers and ensure the cot is put together and used in accordance with guidelines provided by the manufacturer, the BPA believes there are no safety concerns."

Particular care should be taken if you buy a secondhand drop-sided cot or dismantle yours and then re-assemble it for a subsequent baby.

It really isn't an advantage if both sides drop, as the cot will probably be against a wall. Note that very few cot-beds have drop sides.

❊ *An integral teething rail* Many teething babies like to gnaw on their cot rail, which can cause the wood to deteriorate – damaging the cot but probably not your baby. Some cot side rails are covered with non-toxic plastic 'teething rails'. Separate stick-on teething guards can be bought relatively cheaply (Prince Lionheart make them), so if the cot you've set your heart on doesn't have one, don't be put off. Be warned though that these stick-on protectors won't fit on cots with unusually wide rims.

❊ *Castors* These are valuable if you'll move the cot between rooms (check the cot will fit through your doorframes). They also make moving the cot easier so you can clean underneath it. The wheels must be lockable for safety reasons.

Steer clear of...

❊ *Play features* A few cots feature integral 'playbeads' – wooden beads that twirl around. These shouldn't influence your choice either way as more interesting toys are available that can be safely attached to a cot.

BEDSIDE CRIBS AND COTS

These are a wonderful solution if sharing your bed with your baby appeals (research suggests this helps prolong breastfeeding), but you're worried about the risks of smothering or overheating. One side of the crib or cot drops down (although it can be raised if it needs to 'stand alone' sometimes) and the base adjusts level with your mattress forming a 'private wing' of your bed for your baby.

There are various models available which work in different ways; check whether the one you want will be compatible with your style of bed. Some are designed to clip on to bedstead frames and therefore won't work with a divan. Others stand flush alongside the bed but are not physically attached to it – these won't be ideal if your bed has a wide surround. Also note that sometimes the fourth side that allows you to use the crib or cot to 'stand alone' is sold separately and therefore costs extra.

PRODUCT SHOWCASE

The Stokke Sleepi is that distinctive oval-shaped 'cot' you might see in some shops and which, depending on what add-ons you buy, starts off as a crib, converts to a cot and then to a junior bed. If that isn't enough multi-tasking, once the junior bed is outgrown, the Sleepi becomes two chairs or a sofa.

It's very well constructed from solid beech wood and, unlike other cots, needn't be consigned to gather dust in the loft when it's outgrown. On the downside, the kits needed to convert the Sleepi from one 'form' into another cost extra so the 'multi-purposeness' comes at a price. In fact, if you buy the full range from crib to junior bed, it'll set you back over £1000, although that does at least include mattresses.

Bedside Crib or Cot
Troll, Bednest, BabyBay Cot

Bedside cots rarely come as part of a co-ordinated 'room set', so if later on you move yours to the nursery and want matching furniture such as a changing unit and wardrobe, you'll have to do your best to find something that works alongside it.

MATTRESSES

Manufacturers have upped the ante with baby mattresses in recent years, introducing fancy new materials and terminology and mentions of SIDS prevention.

It won't surprise you to learn that while a perfectly adequate standard sprung cot-bed mattress costs around £70, one boasting extra breathability, temperature-controlling features, super-duper air flow functions and so on, can set you back at least double that.

In our opinion, and indeed that of many SIDS experts, there's a fair bit of playing on the fears of expectant parents going on. These premium mattresses are no safer than good-quality standard ones. In fact, if we're talking purely about safety, there are just two unbreakable rules for baby mattresses (whether they are for use in cots or smaller first beds):

* *They must be firm* (Tiny babies can suffocate if they end up face down in a soft mattress).

❋ *They should fit snugly* with a gap of less than 4cm around each edge so there's no chance of your baby's face getting trapped in the gap.

Another thing to flag here is the importance of buying a new mattress. This isn't just a view peddled by the nursery industry to boost sales; the FSID advises that ideally every baby should have a new mattress. If this isn't possible, only use an old one if you know its history and it has a completely waterproof cover with no tears, cracks or holes in it. Clean and dry it thoroughly before use.

If your baby's sleeping place isn't a standard size, most nursery retailers can order tailor-made or 'special-cut' mattresses. These usually won't cost much more but you'll need to allow extra time, as they can take three or four weeks to be made. For a crib or carrycot, which needs a mattress with rounded corners or oval ends, we recommend providing the retailer with a template made from newspaper, so that you get the right shape.

Look for...
Essential
❋ *Firmness.*
❋ *A snug fit in the cot/Moses basket/carrycot.*

Useful
❋ *A waterproof barrier* If your baby does one of the dreaded 'four ps' (pee, poo, posset and puke) in the night, you'll be thankful for a waterproof barrier between the mattress and bedding, allowing you to clean up and get back to bed more quickly. If one of these yucky substances soaks into the mattress, it can take ages to dry out and soggy, unclean mattresses harbour bacteria. A mattress with an integral waterproof cover is useful but you can easily add one (see page 97). Waterproof covers should be breathable; the most basic PVC ones aren't and can get clammy in hot weather, potentially contributing to a baby overheating. Some mattresses have cotton on one side and waterproof material on the other; the cotton side is designed for use in summer

A WORD ABOUT PVC

In the mid-1990s there were concerns about links between PVC mattress covers and cot death, the theory being that when babies' urine makes contact with fire retardants used to treat PVC, toxic compounds are released that contribute to cot death. This theory has now been largely discounted by experts, but most manufacturers still make a big deal about using non-PVC materials for waterproofing mattress coverings.

and the wipeable side for the rest of the time. Babies get sick in hot weather, too, sometimes without warning, so you can bet the very night you turn the mattress over to the cotton side, your baby will develop a bout of vomiting.

❋ *A hypo-allergenic mattress* This is advisable if you are concerned about allergies. An alternative is to use a mattress 'casing' that's impermeable to dust mites (their faeces contribute to allergies) and is also waterproof.

MATTRESS TYPES

Foam

Foam mattresses are relatively cheap and the most basic will simply be a chunk of foam encased in a plastic cover. More sophisticated versions have vents within the foam. Note that if the vents are only at the top they will be fairly useless if your baby is sleeping in the recommended 'feet to foot' position.

The ventilation holes are sometimes covered in mesh and intended to make the mattress more breathable to prevent clamminess or overheating, and to allow moisture such as sweat or regurgitated milk to drain away from a baby. This sounds sensible but the FSID suggests vents make a mattress harder to clean and does not recommend them. One idea is to use a breathable waterproof mattress cover over them – cleanliness shouldn't be a problem and the vents might still be beneficial.

Some pricier foam mattresses have a removable top layer of machine-washable, breathable material making them less clammy and easier to keep clean.

+ Lightweight, so easier to change bedding.
+ Non-allergenic as dust mites can't survive in foam.
+ Less expensive than sprung interior or natural fibre, so particularly good for Moses baskets, carrycots and cribs that might only be used for a matter of weeks.
− Cheaper, thinner mattresses can sag and are not as comfortable for older babies as other options.
− Must be kept covered with a waterproof layer to prevent bacterial growth.

Sprung

These contain a layer of springs, usually encased in foam or coir (see below) and sometimes other materials such as lambs' wool. Covers can be waterproof or heavyweight cotton.

+ More comfortable and supportive than foam for heavier children (so better for cot-beds as these are used for longer).
− More expensive than foam.
− Heavier, so making the bed can be harder work – especially an issue if you've had a caesarean section.

Coir

Coir (natural coconut fibre) is a traditional mattress material, sometimes sandwiched with natural latex, lambs' wool or both. Coir mattresses tend to have natural cotton covers and therefore you'll need to buy a separate waterproof mattress protector (see page 97). Coir is a popular material in the 'greener' mattresses sold by organic baby products specialists.

+ Usually all natural so appealing for parents concerned about chemicals.
+ Supportive and long-lasting. It keeps its shape well and is less likely to sag, so especially good for a cot-bed, which might be used for up to six years.
− Expensive.

In the UK, all mattresses, other than those made of naturally fire-retardant materials such as lambs' wool, must be treated with fire-retardant chemicals. At the time of writing, the Baby Products Association (BPA) is campaigning for baby mattresses to be exempt from fireproofing but for now they aren't. We're not aware of any scientific evidence to suggest fire retardants are harmful, but if you prefer to limit the number of chemicals with which your baby is in contact, you can buy 100% natural mattresses from specialist retailers such as Natural Mat Company and Little Green Sheep (both available online).

Mattress
Rochingham • ✿ Natural
Mat Company, Little
Green Sheep

Verdict: For your baby's cot or cot-bed we suggest investing in a good-quality coir or sprung mattress. For a first bed that might only see a couple of months use or is only for naps, foam should suffice.

Look for...

✳ *A breathable but waterproof cover* If it isn't waterproof, buy a separate mattress protector.

✳ *A mattress that isn't too heavy* Very heavy mattresses mean bed-making will be hard work.

✳ *For foam mattresses*, foam that's thick enough to provide sufficient support and comfort for the baby – at least 8cm in depth for a cot/cot-bed.

BEDDING

Bedding is one of the most jargon-free and relatively simple aspects of baby shopping. We haven't yet seen boasts of 'anti-colic systems' or 'high-tech breathability technology' when it comes to sheets or blankets, although the way the baby industry is going, these could be just around the corner.

The main decision you'll face is whether to go with the traditional 'sheets and blanket' combination or the now popular sleep bags route when tucking your little one up at bedtime (or not, in the case of the latter, as no tucking in is required). Even if you go for sleep bags at bedtime, you will need a few small blankets for the pram.

THE FABULOUS BABY SLEEP BAG

Baby sleep bags might appear to the uninitiated like another new-fangled way to ensure you part with yet more cash when baby shopping but as far as we're concerned, they're one of the baby industry's best inventions.

Made from either T-shirt type jersey, light towelling, woven cotton, merino wool or muslin (organic versions are also available), they're worn like little coats that zip down the front or are fastened with poppers at the shoulders but are closed at the bottom and usually sleeveless to help prevent overheating.

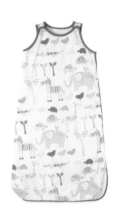

Note that bags must be the right size for your baby (they come in age and weight ranges) so her head can't slip down through the neck hole. Normal nightclothes are worn underneath, according to the weight of the bag and the room temperature.

There are plenty of baby product options where the answer to the question 'which is best?' is 'it depends' but this isn't one of them. As far as we're concerned (and so, too, our parent panel), there's no debate – sleep bags beat conventional baby bedding hands down.

The only exception is during the first few weeks when some newborns benefit from swaddling (see page 98).

Why do we like sleep bags so much? Well, it's all ultimately about maximising the chances of you and your baby getting a decent night's sleep – need we say more?!

The main benefits

❉ Unlike blankets, they can't get kicked off in the night; even young babies wriggle around and knock their covers off, exposing their little limbs to the cold and causing unnecessary waking.

❉ They mean less worrying about how much bedding a baby needs or what she should wear to bed. Bags come with tog ratings (see page 92) to give an indication of warmth, whereas blankets are of varying thicknesses and materials so temperature guidelines saying 'use two blankets if the nursery is x degrees' can be misleading.

❉ When travelling, they take up less space in luggage and are familiar even if the cot and room in which your baby sleeps are not.

❉ Your baby remains nice and warm during night feeds because she can stay in her bag (although some can be fiddly for night-time nappy changes).

❉ Perhaps most importantly of all, there's no worrying about blankets ending up over your baby's head.

� Adventurous toddlers can be prevented from climbing out of their cot (potentially injuring themselves) if they wear sleep bags, thereby delaying the move to a proper bed. For older

Merino wool sleep bags are more expensive than those made of other materials, but are 'temperature regulating' so one bag can be used all year round without the need for different tog ratings. If you buy them sized 0–2 years, rather than in smaller age bands, in the long run, the overall cost will be about the same as if you bought cheaper materials.

babies, the bag should be 'escape proof' with the zip ending at the bottom rather than the top. Some bags have two zips for extra security; you can also put a bag on back to front to make the zip harder for an older baby to undo. Check zips and fastenings won't irritate your baby if, when she is older, she chooses to sleep on her tummy.

How much do they cost?

Those on a tight budget are sometimes put off sleep bags as they're perceived as more expensive than blankets – they used to cost at least £20 to £25 each – and you need two or three sizes to cover the baby and toddler years. Recently, however, supermarkets like Asda and Tesco and discount retailers have been offering them for as little as £10 each (although sometimes these don't display a tog rating). Most parents who've tried them think sleep bags are well worth any extra money compared to blankets and we firmly agree.

When do you need them?

Although you can use some sleep bags from birth, most are not suitable for smaller newborns and there's an argument that for very new babies, blankets and sheets are better for the first few weeks as they allow you to swaddle, and provide more flexibility to add and remove layers.

Our suggestion is that if your baby will initially sleep in a smaller first bed, start off with pram-sized sheets and blankets and switch to sleep bags after a month or so. The blankets you buy won't be wasted as you can still use them in the pram. If you plan to introduce sleep bags at some stage, it makes sense to do so before your baby moves to a proper cot, to avoid buying a full set of cot-sized blankets and top sheets as well.

If you'd prefer to use sleep bags from day one, it's safe to do so if you ensure the bag is the right weight for the room temperature and the correct size for your baby. We've found that some bags labelled 0–12 months are really better suited to babies from three months, so choose a newborn one and check it against your baby to make doubly sure it fits (crucially the neck hole mustn't be so big your baby's head could slip down into the bag).

The smallest size of the best-known brand, Grobag (sometimes used generically by parents as a synonym for sleep bags), is 0–6 months, which is suitable for babies weighing 4 kg (8 lb 8 oz) upwards.

Tog ratings

Most baby sleep bags are labelled with a tog rating indicating the warmth they provide. These can seem surprisingly low – an adult duvet might be 10 or 13 togs, baby sleep bags are usually either1 or 2.5 togs. Don't worry, 2.5 togs are perfectly adequate for a baby even in winter, and you can always add an extra layer of nightclothes underneath. (Most winter-weight bags have a polyester filling but some are 100% cotton.)

When choosing bags, bear in mind the season in which they are to be used. For spring, summer and autumn, buy 1 tog (1 tog bags also work well year round for daytime naps if your baby is fully dressed). For winter, buy 2.5 togs unless the nursery is quite warm in which case 1 tog should suffice.

Summer-weight 0.5 tog bags are also available and are great for very warm weather, holidays or visits to the grandparents if, like ours, they insist on keeping the house heated to tropical temperatures at all times.

How many?

Buy at least two sleep bags, three if you can afford it (one on, one in the wash and a spare clean one in case of accidents).

Look for…
Essential

- ❋ *No sleeves or hood* Sleeves are not necessary for a baby sleep bag; only buy one with sleeves if the sleeves can be removed to prevent overheating. Hoods are a complete no-no as your baby's head should be uncovered in bed.
- ❋ *Washability* Choose bags that are washable at 40° or more and can go in the tumble dryer.
- ❋ *A secure fastening* Some bags zip down the front, others have poppers on the shoulders and a zip around the edge. Younger babies need their nappies changing in the night, so check you'll be able to undo the bottom of the bag only.

Sleep Bag
££ Grobag

£ Ikea · ££ ✿ Green Baby and Little Green Sheep · £££ Merino Kids and Bambino Merino (temperature regulating merino wool); aden and anais (muslin)

Useful

❖ *A tog rating* so you have a better idea of the warmth it will provide and the clothes needed underneath.

❖ *Car seat harness compatibility* If you think you will travel by car a lot after bedtime, these allow you to transfer your baby to and from the car and cot with less disturbance.

BLANKETS

There are some gorgeous baby blankets on the market but these are a popular gift for newborns so don't be tempted to buy too many. Above all else, a baby blanket needs to be washable. Don't even think of buying one that has to be dry cleaned or hand washed no matter how beautiful it is.

The four main fabrics

❖ *Cellular cotton* Traditionally, this loosely woven 'holey' material has been the most popular for baby blankets; loose-weave blankets are cool in summer and warm in winter. However, if the holes are too big, little fingers and toes can get caught. Light and breathable, these blankets help prevent overheating and are good for layering.

❖ *Cellular acrylic* Sometimes a cotton/acrylic mix is used, which is warmer than cellular cotton but not as gentle for sensitive skin.

WHAT BEDDING DO BABIES NEED ACCORDING TO THE ROOM'S TEMPERATURE?

Room temperature	Traditional bedding	Sleeping bag tog rating
24°C (75° F)	Sheet only	0.5 tog
21°C (70°F)	Sheet + one layer* of blankets	1 tog
18° C (65°F)	Sheet + two layers* of blankets	2.5 togs
16°C (60° F)	Sheet + three layers* of blankets	2.5 togs + one layer of blankets

*One blanket folded in two is equivalent to two layers of blankets

* *Fleece* Super soft, easy to wash and quick drying, this is usually too warm for the nursery but ideal in the pram or pushchair if it's very cold.
* *Wool* is also nice and warm so useful for the pram or pushchair on cold days but ensure the blankets are machine washable as not all wool is.

Babies under 12 months of age shouldn't sleep with pillows or quilts.

Do you really need them?
You will need a few small blankets for the pram or pushchair even if you'll use sleep bags at bedtime.

When do you need them?
From birth.

How many?
* Three lighter weight blankets in Moses basket or crib size (only two if you are going to use sleep bags from birth).
* One or two wool or fleecy pram blankets (only one if you buy a cosytoe or footmuff [see page 122]) for very cold days. Any lighter blankets you use in a smaller first bed can also be used in the pram or pushchair in warmer weather.
* Three or four in cot/cot-bed size (only one if you're using sleep bags); you can use one as a back-up extra layer if it's exceptionally cold.

We don't recommend buying any small 'receiving' blankets, as we think shaped swaddling wraps are easier to use when wrapping up newborns (see page 98).

Sheets
Regular: DK, John Lewis, Ikea • ✿ Green Baby, Little Green Sheep

SHEETS
Fitted sheets (those with elasticated 'shaped' corners and sometimes also with elasticated sides) make better bottom sheets than flat ones because they're less likely to wrinkle or come away from the mattress when your baby moves around, and making the bed with them is easier. Check the size of fitted sheets needed for your cot or cot-bed as mattress dimensions vary.

If you aren't going to use sleep bags, you'll also need flat top sheets to layer with blankets. If you have an unusually sized cot or crib, flat sheets may be your only option as correctly

Many retailers now stock organic baby bedding made from cotton or bamboo that was grown without pesticides or chemicals. Although they do cost a bit more, organic products are usually softer next to delicate newborn skin.

If you'll use both a Moses basket and a carrycot, buy pram-size sheets for both rather than any Moses basket ones. The pram sheets might be a little baggy in the basket but you'll appreciate not having to sort out which is which after laundering as the size difference is so minimal.

sized fitted sheets may not be available. Flat sheets can also come in useful if, 12 months or so later, you move from sleep bags to a quilt or duvet for your cot, as having a flat sheet between your baby and the quilt or duvet can reduce how often you need to wash the thicker top cover.

The four main fabrics

❊ **Woven cotton** is cool for summer.
❊ **Flannelette**, or brushed cotton, is warm in winter.
❊ **Terry** is thin cotton/'cotton mix' towelling, which is usually stretchy.
❊ **Cotton jersey** This stretchy T-shirt-type material is used for fitted sheets only.

For fitted bottom sheets, we recommend cotton jersey. Their stretchiness makes bed-making easy and they fit snugly even if your mattress is not quite a standard size.

If you're buying top sheets for a Moses basket, crib or carrycot, which will only be used for a few months, flannelette is a good choice for a winter newborn and woven cotton for a summer baby.

Top sheets for a cot or cot-bed will be used in all seasons, so woven cotton is probably your best bet.

When do you need them?

You'll need sheets for your baby's initial bed ready for the birth. If you aren't using a cot from birth, cot sheets can be bought later on.

How many?

❊ Three to four fitted sheets, and an optional three to four flat (unnecessary if using shaped swaddling blankets, see page 98, or sleep bags from birth) for the Moses basket, carrycot or crib in 'pram' or 'crib' size. The latter are readily available in nursery shops but not usually found in general bedding stores. Obviously these won't be necessary if your baby sleeps in a cot from day one.
❊ Three to four fitted sheets in cot/cot-bed size, and if you aren't using sleep bags, three to four flat ones, too.

Our recommended quantities are based on the idea of one sheet on, one in the wash, one ready to go and, if you choose, one more spare.

MATTRESS PROTECTORS

If your chosen mattress doesn't have a waterproof cover, it's essential to add one as soggy bedding is inevitable at some stage with a baby and clearing up will be a lot easier if nothing unpleasant has soaked through to the mattress. A breathable waterproof under-sheet is best. Waterproofing will stop the mattress getting wet or stained, and breathability will help prevent overheating and clamminess.

Not all waterproof covers are the 'crinkly' variety; modern brushed cotton ones don't feel like plastic at all, as their waterproof layer of polyurethane is encased in two layers of softer cotton.

How many?

Two in pram/crib size and two in cot/cot-bed size.

If you buy flat rather than fitted protectors, these can also be used during potty training to stop little accidents soaking into the mattress and over the top of your baby's normal sheets during any bouts of vomiting. Likewise, pram-sized flat protectors for a carrycot, crib or Moses basket can double as portable changing mats and as protection for car seats and buggies during potty training.

SHEEPSKINS

Research quoted in journals like *The Lancet* has shown that sheepskin has a calming effect on newborns and regulates body temperature, since it is warm in winter but cool in summer. Sheepskins are even used in some hospital special care baby units; studies suggest that babies who use them gain weight more readily.

There have been worries about a link with cot death in the past but the FSID's latest advice is that sleeping on a sheepskin is OK as long as your baby sleeps on her back.

Once your baby learns to roll on to her front, she should no longer sleep on the sheepskin. It can, however, still be used as a floor mat for sitting, playing or lounging on.

 **Mattress Protectors**
DK, Hippychick,
B. Sensible

Look for...

✳ *A sheepskin specifically for babies.*
✳ *Washability* Cleaning baby vomit from a sheepskin's fibres with a cloth is a tough task. Sheepskin shampoos are available for machine washing.

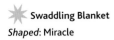 Swaddling Blanket
Shaped: Miracle

 *Shaped:* Merino Kids
Cocooi, Swaddle Up,
Grobag • *Non-shaped:*
aden and anais

OTHER BEDTIME PRODUCTS

SWADDLING WRAPS/BLANKETS

Loosely securing a baby in a blanket is a time-honoured way to calm a newborn and help her feel more secure. Newborns often become startled by the unintentional movement of their own arms and legs, which are due to the Moro or startle reflex. Swaddling keeps limbs tucked away and also exerts gentle pressure on the stomach to ease wind. It's something many parents swear by for their newborn (although a few babies don't like it at all).

Any thin blanket or large muslin can be used for swaddling but wrapping the blanket correctly can be frustratingly tricky, especially when a wriggly baby doesn't want to co-operate. Shaped swaddling blankets make it easier and are usually of an appropriate weight to avoid overheating. Choose a breathable, lightweight and washable fabric.

Swaddling blankets can provide an excellent stopgap before introducing sleep bags and we certainly recommend swaddling if your newborn is hard to settle.

How many?

Start off with one, see if your baby responds well to swaddling and, if so, buy a couple extra.

PRODUCT SHOWCASE

If your baby doesn't seem to like having her arms wrapped up, you could always leave them outside the swaddle, but there's also a product called the **Swaddle Up** – a little like a snug sleep bag crossed with a swaddle blanket. This allows the arms to rest up beside the head, which is a sleeping position many newborns naturally choose.

BUMPERS

These fabric-covered pads tie on to the bars of the cot or crib, making the sides softer if your baby ends up squashed against them. They also stop little limbs dangling out of the side of the cot and prevent dummies falling out. Finally, they sometimes allow you to sneak out of the nursery unnoticed if your baby wants you around while she's dozing off – with a bumper in place, your early exit is less likely to be noticed! But conversely, if you want to take a quick peek at your baby to check on her, without her seeing you, they make that harder as you can't peer in from a distance.

Another problem is that the window of time when they add to a baby's comfort is very short because once your little one starts sitting confidently and begins to be able to pull herself up, they must be removed, as they can aid a more adventurous toddler trying to climb out of her cot.

Even more seriously, they've been linked to a number of deaths of babies in the US. Some of these incidents involved accidental strangulations with long bumper ties, others were caused by babies ending up with their faces against the bumper and suffocating.

Before automatically striking bumpers off your shopping list, you need to consider the following. In the UK, trading standards for bumper ties ensure these are too short to be a strangulation risk. As regards suffocation, we consulted the Baby Products Association who said they were not aware of any cases of this occurring in recent years in Europe and that bumpers are safe to use until a baby can sit up unaided. This could be because most bumpers available here tend to be much smaller – called half bumpers – and only go around a

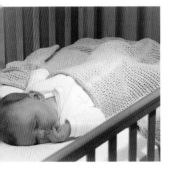

If you do buy a conventional bumper, check the ties regularly to ensure they are secure. In the past, there were concerns that bumpers could contribute to a baby overheating but recent research suggests they're neither good nor bad. Remove the bumper from your baby's cot once she starts pulling herself up.

small part of the cot. (In the US, they have typically been full bumpers, fitting around every side.)

If you feel concerned though, given the limited benefit of having a cot bumper, you probably should steer clear – they are more a decorative accessory and none of the issues they seek to prevent are that serious.

Should you find that, once your baby is rolling or shuffling around her cot, she ends up with her arms through the bars or is flinging her dummy out, have a look at the newer styles of bumper, which seek to address safety concerns.

The two main new-style bumper options

❋ *Bumpers which Velcro® on to each individual cot bar* such as the Hippychick Bumpster, have no ties to worry about, and because there are gaps between them (albeit narrower ones than without a bumper), they allow air to circulate. However, they are made from the same sort of filled fabric that traditional bumpers feature, so if you are concerned about suffocation, these still probably won't be for you.

❋ *Those made from thinner, breathable mesh fabrics* stop little limbs getting stuck between cot bars or dummies falling out, yet let air circulate more, can be breathed through and are supposed to collapse down if an older baby tries to climb on to them. Examples include Purflo and AirWrap.

COT SEPARATORS OR DIVIDERS

These are small firm bolsters that fit horizontally across the cot between the side rails, separating the mattress into two sections. They're extendable to suit different cot widths.

Cot separators or dividers are usually marketed as safety aids to keep your baby in the 'feet-to-foot' position (her feet should be at the foot of her cot and her bedding should reach no higher than her armpits so she can't wriggle down under it.

In our opinion (and more importantly, the FSID's), separators or dividers are unnecessary. If you use sleep bags there's no need to keep a baby in the feet-to-foot position as there are no blankets to wriggle under anyway. Even if you do use blankets, tucking your baby in well in the feet-to-foot position is easy to do and sufficient precaution.

Where a divider can be useful is if you have twins and want them to start off sleeping in the same cot but in a space of their own.

CAT AND MOSQUITO NETS

These fit over a baby's sleeping place to stop cats and insects getting to your little one while she sleeps.

Cat nets are stronger and quite rigid, whereas mosquito ones are typically made of a lighter, finer weave material. Even if you think your darling cat wouldn't hurt a flea, do get a cat net as there have been rare cases where cats have climbed into a cot, snuggled up next to a baby for a cuddle and sadly, the baby has suffocated.

Note that cat nets must be taut across the top of the cot or other baby sleeping place, as otherwise the net could collapse if the cat climbs on top of it.

SLEEP POSITIONERS

Look through some of the specialist baby catalogues and you'll come across assorted baby 'sleep positioners'.

The three main types

* *Those designed to keep babies on their backs* These prevent a baby rolling over, but are unnecessary and not recommended by the FSID. If your baby is put to bed on her back from birth, she'll be used to that position and, once she's old enough to roll over, be strong enough to sleep on her tummy or side.
* *Those designed to keep babies on their sides* These are intended to prevent flat head syndrome (plagiocephaly). We aren't keen on these either. Flat-head syndrome is where a baby develops a flat patch on the back of her head but this doesn't normally cause discomfort and usually rights itself. The safest sleeping position for a newborn is on her back and the only exception is where a baby has specific health issues and a doctor advises you that she should sleep on her side or stomach. If this is the case with your baby, ask your doctor about the best way of achieving that. You can help prevent flat spots by encouraging plenty of 'tummy time'

out of the cot or using a baby-safe memory foam pillow such as those made by Cuski.

❖ *Wedge-shaped positioners*, which usually consist of a foam wedge that sits on top of the mattress, are designed to elevate a baby's head and shoulders. These can be effective at reducing reflux and easing congestion if a baby has a cold. Try putting something sturdy like a couple of hardback books under the head end of your cot to raise it before buying one of these positioners as the books might work just as well. If you do buy a positioner, it should be very firm to avoid any risk of suffocation.

QUILTS, DUVETS AND COVERLETS

Your baby should not use a quilt or duvet as bedding until she is older than 12 months, by which time you might be happily using sleep bags and reluctant to make the switch to a quilt or duvet anyway.

Coverlets are lighter in weight and most are labelled suitable for use from 3.5 kg (7 lb 7 oz) – around the average baby's birth weight. They're usually equivalent to a top sheet and fleece blanket but they offer less flexibility for adding or removing layers and we favour sleep bags anyway.

If you are tempted by a quilt that matches the rest of your nursery range, all is not lost as it can be used as a floor mat for your baby to sit or lie upon. Don't, however, drape it over the side of the cot while your baby is within; it might look nice but could slip off on to your sleeping baby's head.

NURSERY FURNITURE AND DECORATION

A MATTER OF TASTE

Your baby doesn't need a beautifully decorated nursery to be happy, but for many parents, sorting out their impending arrival's room is a pregnancy rite of passage.

That said, a nursery might not get slept in for the first months; if you follow safe sleeping advice, your baby will be in your bedroom with you at night and the nursery will remain largely a place to keep all his paraphernalia and clothing. Yet, regardless, it still makes sense to get your baby's room ready before his birth, because afterwards, as you'll have worked out by now, life will get too hectic for self-assembly furniture and trips to DIY shops.

SHOPPING LIST

✓ Cot/cot-bed, *see page 82*
✓ Storage – drawers, wardrobe or both
? Changing unit
? A comfortable chair for feeding
? Finishing touches
? Blackout curtains or blinds, or blackout cot canopy
? New lighting

NURSERY STORAGE

This will probably represent a major portion of your baby shopping budget and like the cot, contributes considerably to the look of the nursery. Although there are a few good-quality bargains out there, generally with nursery furniture you do get what you pay for.

Do you really need it?

You will need somewhere to store your baby's things although it need not be specific nursery furniture – any wardrobe and drawers will do.

When do you need it?

It can be useful to have the furniture set up before the birth so all your baby's kit is organised ready for his arrival. If this isn't possible, it really won't be the end of the world if you sort it out later on. Consider that some furniture has to be ordered well in advance – up to three months before delivery – so if you do want to get everything sorted before the big day, start shopping when you're around six months pregnant.

✳**Nursery Furniture**
£ Ikea • ££ John Lewis, Cosatto, East Coast, Kub Nursery, Izziwotnot, Europe Baby • £££ Stokke, Kidsmill, Boori, Silver Cross, Bambizi

What will you need?

✳ *Plenty of storage space* Baby things are small but numerous and as babies grow, so does the amount of stuff they acquire. Drawers are essential – either within a changing unit (see below) or separately. They're useful not only for stowing clothes but also for nappies, wipes, muslins, toiletries and general kit. A wardrobe is useful but not essential initially. Baby and toddler clothes are small, so if you do get a wardrobe, you could increase capacity by adding a second hanging rail halfway down.

Look for...

✳ *Something that's well built* Units should be able to withstand the bashings of a boisterous toddler. Solid wood is more expensive than veneer but will last better. If possible, avoid items made of chipboard, plywood and particleboard, which are made by bonding wood chips, plant fibres or

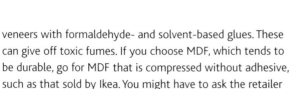

veneers with formaldehyde- and solvent-based glues. These
can give off toxic fumes. If you choose MDF, which tends to
be durable, go for MDF that is compressed without adhesive,
such as that sold by Ikea. You might have to ask the retailer
for information on the item's construction as it won't always
be provided in product literature.

❊ **Longevity** Furniture needn't be baby sized; your child will
need help getting dressed for the foreseeable future anyway,
so don't worry about whether he'll be able to reach into his
cupboards when aged two or three. You can always add an
extra, lower hanging rail to a full-sized wardrobe.

❊ **Drawers with built-in stoppers** These prevent older babies
and toddlers dragging drawers out of the unit and dropping
them, potentially on their own feet.

Bear in mind when choosing nursery furniture, that something
that looks cute for a baby might seem out of place in an older
child's room. Somehow this is especially so for boys' bedrooms
– older girls are less likely to mind those sweet, cut-out hearts.

A CHANGING UNIT

These aren't vital but can be the saviour of a bad back if
changing nappies on a mat on the floor is a strain. A unit also
helps keep changing kit tidy and close to hand. Some parents
use one throughout the nappy years; others abandon it and
use the floor once their baby gets mobile because they are
worried about their baby rolling off. Cot-top changers save
space in the more compact and bijou nursery, although they're
a pain to lift on and off the cot.

Some units are open-shelved, others have drawers and/or
cupboards underneath. The latter cost more but have greater
longevity, acting as storage beyond the nappy-changing phase.
Avoid the 'bath dresser' variety (see page 45). Worth
considering is Ikea's Sniglar open changing unit, great value at
around £25 – it isn't the sturdiest but will do the job.

NURSERY/NURSING CHAIRS

A nursing chair is specially designed as a comfortable place to
feed your baby, often with the option of adding a footstool.

If nursery space is at a premium, look for furniture ranges offering under-cot drawers for extra storage.

PRODUCT SHOWCASE

The middle ground between traditional and expensive could be the **Kensington Breastfeeding Chair** designed by Dr Lynn Jones. This is more widely affordable and still attractive but it doesn't glide or rock. It does, however, feature an inflatable lumbar back support and is ergonomically designed for breastfeeding, with no sides, so you can wrap a feeding cushion (see page 64) around you to support your baby. Worth considering if you like its style.

Many provide a rocking motion to lull little ones (and parents!) to sleep but you can usually fix them into position if you prefer. Such armchairs also provide a cosy bedtime story spot well beyond the feeding days.

On the other hand, you can, of course, feed your baby in bed or in a normal armchair, especially if you use a feeding pillow for support. Additionally, if the chair is in the nursery and your baby is sleeping in your room for the first months, it might not be that appealing to switch rooms, given you could just do the feed in your bed.

Purpose-designed nursing chairs fall into two categories; if we were being brutal these would be 'naff' (many look like they'd fit in well in a retirement home) and 'chic but expensive'! Chairs from the likes of Olli Ella certainly wouldn't look out of place on the pages of a stylish interiors magazine but cost upwards of £800 – beyond most budgets. If you can stretch your finances to it though, investing in one of their feeding chairs is something you probably won't regret.

The best way to insulate yourself from making a mistake buy is to ensure that you actually like the nursing chair enough to have it in your house regardless of its function. If you look at traditional-style chairs and can picture one in your home, check out those made by companies such as Kub and Tutti Bambini. Until recently there was also a brand called Dutailier, whose versions were particularly well made (although no more attractive!), but they have now gone out of business. You might, however, be able to secure a secondhand one.

FINISHING DECORATIVE TOUCHES

Some parents revel in creating a fully themed and co-ordinated nursery, others take the view that for the first year or two their baby won't care if the walls are plain or the 'wrong' colour. Let's face it, baby girls with blue walls in their nursery aren't likely to be psychologically damaged by the experience.

An effective middle ground is to use a neutral paint on walls, adding pictures or wall stickers and accessories to create a theme. This will cost less and can be changed more easily once your no-longer-so-little-one finds wall-to-ceiling Winnie the Pooh a tad embarrassing when schoolmates come over.

Tips on decoration

❋ If you're redecorating the nursery, do it well before your baby will spend time in there to limit exposure to fumes from paint strippers and paints. As it's not advisable for you to be exposed to these fumes during pregnancy, have someone else decorate the nursery (taking the opportunity to put your feet up while he or she gets on with it!). The Nursery Paint Company's products are more expensive than your average tin of Dulux but worth a look as they're all natural and come in a lovely range of colours.

❋ Whichever brand you go for, choose a durable paint finish – toddlers don't tend to respect paintwork.

❋ Think about longevity when choosing designs and patterns; avoid anything too babyish.

❋ Wall stickers (also known as 'decals') are a cheap way to add a theme, which you can change later on with little effort. Look for self-adhesive ones that can be removed easily. Try wallglamour.co.uk, walliescutouts.co.uk, Wall Candy, Next, Bambizi, Brightroomdesigns.co.uk, FuntoSee, bouf.com.

PRODUCT SHOWCASE

Content & Calm Cot Canopy This is a special 'blackout' cover, which fits over a standard cot, cot-bed or travel cot, making the inside dark. It's ideal if you can't or don't want to fit blackout blinds to the nursery or to your bedroom, or when travelling and you are sharing with your baby and want to be able to read in bed with the light on, without worrying about disturbing your child. Snoozeshade also have a similar product.

BLINDS AND CURTAINS

Blackout curtains or blinds help many babies to sleep better when it's light outside and will be worth every penny if they mean you get to sleep later on summer mornings because the nursery remains dark. You can buy separate blackout linings to add to existing curtains if you aren't buying new ones. Generally we find blinds more effective than curtains as the latter still allow light through at the top and bottom.

If your child is particularly susceptible to waking from the early morning sun, you can also buy portable blackout blinds, which fix, with suction cups or via static, on to any window up to a certain size; these can be helpful when travelling. Examples are the Gro Anywhere Blind, Lights Out Blind and Magic Blackout Blind.

A cot canopy like the Content & Calm one featured above, is an alternative to blinds as well as an excellent buy for travel if you'll all be in one bedroom or your baby's in a room with flimsy curtains; it could buy you an extra bit of sleep on light summer mornings!

☀ **Night Light**
Moonlight (excellent low-energy plug-in, which costs under £1 a year to run even if on all the time); **Brother Max** (plugs in but innovatively still allows you to use the same socket for other electrical items)

LIGHTING

The key to nursery lighting is flexibility. There will be times when you want a dim light to reassure your baby but not keep him awake, other occasions when you need a little more light but not too much as for night feeds, and still others when only full-on brightness will do, perhaps so you can see to read a bedtime story at the toddler stage.

The ideal solution may be to fit a dimmer switch to the nursery's main light as this way you'll be able to control the

PRODUCT SHOWCASE

The **Babytec Autofade** bedside lamp fades out over a period of time, so your child is gently eased into a darker environment. It's also valuable for night feeds as, in addition to the 'auto fade' function, it can be used as a regular bedside lamp with a dimmer switch.

level of brightness with just one fixture, but this may not work or be possible for all rooms.

There are lots of night lights available – some integral to baby monitors, others separate – but do bear in mind that most provide little more than a reassuring glow for your baby and certainly not enough to prevent you tripping over half a dozen toys if you go into the nursery in the night. A multi-purpose lamp, like the one featured in the product showcase, above, might be a better solution.

TOY BOX
You might want to buy a toy box or two in which to hide all your baby's playthings away. If you do go for one with a lid, check that it has safety or slow-closing hinges (these stop the lid falling shut on to tiny fingers). Other options for toy storage include Tubtrugs, and those general plastic storage tubs sold in DIY shops, such as Homebase and B&Q.

COT MOBILE
See toys and playing chapter, page 159.

DECORATIVE ACCESSORIES
If you want to go the whole hog with everything from co-ordinating nappy tidies to frilly aprons and canopies for the cot, that's your call, but they are not essential and are extra items to clean; some won't be in use for very long.

PRAMS, PUSHCHAIRS, SLINGS AND CARRIERS

PUSHCHAIRS

When we asked our parent panel which purchase they agonised over most, the pushchair was top of the list. But why is selecting a baby's first wheels such a headache? It's probably due to a combination of too much choice, pushchairs having become something of a fashion statement, and the fact that the perfect pushchair doesn't exist, so looking for it is futile. Given these reasons, some parents acquire a whole fleet – the ownership record among our friends is five at once! Other people become serial buyers – buying one, flogging it (in the hope of acquiring something better), buying another, and so on.

SHOPPING LIST

✓ Pram/buggy with a lie-flat seat or carrycot
  (*unless using a sling/carrier all the time*)
✓ Rain cover
? Footmuff
? Sunshade and insect net *(for summer/holidays)*
? Buggy weights
? Sling/carrier
? Cat net *(essential if you have a cat)*
✗ Pram parasol

PUSHCHAIR TERMINOLOGY

❋ *Pram* Although sometimes used generically for all types of baby wheels, strictly speaking this refers to a model with a carrycot.

❋ *Buggy or stroller* A lightweight pushchair with a semi-upright or upright seat (it might recline).

❋ *Travel system* A pushchair that accommodates an infant car seat. A model with 'travel system' as part of the name usually comes with a compatible car seat included (be sure to check it fits your vehicle before buying). Many other pushchairs can be turned into a travel system with the addition of a compatible car seat.

❋ *Two-in-ones/Three-in-ones* A chassis plus either a seat that reclines into a pram-style unit for a newborn but sits upright *(a 'two-in-one')* or a carrycot and pushchair seat *('three-in-one')* for use later on.

❋ *Umbrella-folding buggy* A lightweight, compact buggy, which when folded, is long and narrow like an umbrella.

❋ *Telescopic-folding buggy* A buggy, which when folded, is shorter and wider than an umbrella-folding buggy so is sometimes better for smaller car boots.

❋ *Reversible seats* The direction the pushchair seat faces can be switched between facing the person pushing *('parent facing')* or outwards *('forward facing')*.

The advent of the 'must-have pram'

Pram purchases have become much more style-led recently. If pushing a chic-looking buggy or the celeb mums' current favourite appeals to you, that's fine but don't be seduced solely by style – check for practicality, too. Conversely, don't dismiss a stylish pram, assuming that because it looks flashy, it won't perform well; some of our favourites score high on both counts.

Consider that newborns should ideally lie flat...

The optimal position for newborns is lying fully flat at 180 degrees. This is better for spine development and breathing but not all newborn pushchairs offer this. (Be aware that UK standards on what constitutes 'suitable from birth' models differ from those in the EU and the US; they are less stringent than elsewhere in Europe and stricter than in the US.)

Fundamentally you have three options for a newborn (some models offer more than one of these):

* **A carrycot** *that attaches to a chassis* A carrycot is undoubtedly the best way to allow your newborn to lie properly flat and should ideally be your starting point. Although a carrycot pram will only suit your baby for the first four to six months and might be expensive, most models convert to buggies later on (sometimes referred to as 'three-in-ones') and a detachable carrycot can double as a sleeping place, meaning you can skip buying a crib or Moses basket (but you do need to make sure the mattress is suitable for overnight sleeping, see page 86).

* **A** *'two-in-one' pushchair that's 'suitable from birth'* Some pushchairs recline sufficiently to be labelled 'suitable from birth' under British Standards although this doesn't necessarily mean they lie fully flat. For the health reasons already mentioned, we advocate that only seats that lie fully flat or nearly so are really suitable for newborns for anything beyond short periods. Moreover, buggy seats can be flimsy and not as padded or supportive as a carrycot (though adding a sheepskin pushchair liner might help). If a 'suitable from birth' pushchair is your only option for practical reasons, check how much the seat reclines and go for the one that lies flattest.

* **A** *travel system* This is an infant car seat attached to the pushchair chassis (usually using adaptors) or clipped on to the pushchair seat. Many parents appreciate being able to whisk a car seat straight on to the pushchair, since this avoids waking a baby who has fallen asleep in the car. However, an infant carrier's upright position is not ideal for a baby's spinal and respiratory development. Although it usually protects a baby involved in a car accident better than a lie-flat seat, out of the car, lying flat is preferable. And in reality, most newborns fall back to sleep quickly in the pushchair anyway even if they wake when being transferred. If the ability to place the car seat straight on to the pushchair is something you really want or you regularly take taxis, then ideally go for a lie-flat infant carrier (see page 138).

Travel system packages sometimes involve a compromise because either the pushchair or the car seat sold with it isn't the best choice for you (not all car seats fit all cars).

...but think longer term, too

A common pitfall of this pushchair palaver is focusing overly on the newborn phase, rather than considering longer-term needs. Too many parents invest in a bulky and expensive contraption that's lovely and secure for their newborn, but gets traded in for a more practical, lightweight buggy once their baby hits six months. The result – a costly first set of wheels gets sent to the pushchair graveyard and if it cost, say £500, that works out at an alarming £80+ a month. If you'd prefer one pushchair to last through to toddlerhood, think of both the newborn and toddler stages. For later on, you'll probably want a seat with some recline (it needn't be fully flat) on a light, manoeuvrable buggy that folds easily.

One idea is to start with the upfront intention of buying two pushchair: first choosing something not too expensive, with a comfy lie-flat carrycot for the first months, then trading it for a smaller, lighter-weight option once your baby reaches six months. This means there's no need to compromise at either stage and this scenario sometimes works out cheaper overall if you choose carefully.

When to buy

You won't need a pram the day your baby is born, but soon after you'll probably want to head out for some fresh air. It makes sense to order one before the birth because if your preferred choice is out of stock, you might have to wait up to eight weeks for delivery. It's a good idea to assemble the pram (if needed) and familiarise yourself with it before your new arrival turns up and turns your life upside down.

Take a test drive

Many retailers let you wheel pushchairs around the store and sometimes outside. Take a few for a spin to check how particular models 'handle'; fold them up, put the carrycot/car seat on and off the chassis and test out key features like the brakes.

Best All-rounder
BabyJogger City Mini

Best Budget Buy
Petite Star Zia

Be wary of buying a very newly launched model – some have teething troubles at first so it's better to stick with something tried and tested.

Undoubtedly it's wise to invest time in choosing a buggy; this is one of the most expensive baby purchases you'll make and one of the easiest to mess up. But don't become obsessed with the pursuit of the perfect pram; no pram can possibly tick every box, so prioritise those features that matter to you most and be prepared to sacrifice some of the minor ones.

The main factors to consider in making a decision

When choosing a buggy it's crucial to think about your lifestyle. If several factors are important to you, you might need to compromise or invest in two prams for different situations (perhaps one or both could be bought secondhand to save money).

Be honest with yourself; an all-terrain pram for cross-country walks with your baby might appeal, but it will be far from ideal if your hiking expeditions usually involve strolling to Starbucks to grab a latte. Consider:

Your home

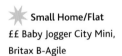

Small Home/Flat
££ Baby Jogger City Mini, Britax B-Agile

If you only have a couple of steps to scale, something sturdy with big rear wheels and a decent suspension can be bumped carefully up and down with your baby in it.

If you live in an upstairs flat and can't leave a pushchair in the lobby, your best bet is a lightweight, easy-fold model. We

---

MONEY-SAVING TIPS FOR PUSHCHAIR PURCHASERS

✳ *Buy 'nearly new'* Some people's serial pram-buying habits provide rich pickings for others wanting a barely-used secondhand model. There's a healthy market for secondhand prams, so have a look at parenting websites for sale sections, NCT 'nearly new' sales, eBay, car boot sales or www.pushchairtrader.co.uk.

✳ *Check out last season's ranges* Most manufacturers change fabrics and colours once or twice a year. You might find old models at a discount. A savvy shop assistant will know when new ranges launch and when old models get marked down.

✳ *Look after your pushchair with a view to selling it* once you've finished with it.

✳ *Don't be pressured* You don't have to buy the equivalent of a Ferrari if a Ford will do.

hate to say it but even this won't be easy, as you'll have to fold and carry it, plus baby, upstairs, along with any bags.

If your home lacks storage space, a compact two-in-one that's freestanding when folded is probably your best bet.

Where you'll go
Rough ground

If you'll frequently push the buggy along bumpy pathways, cross-country or on the beach, an all-terrain pushchair will be a must rather than a fashion accessory. Decent suspension and large pneumatic wheels make pushing over rough ground easier. Some all-terrain prams now have foam-filled wheels, which offer the best of both worlds – a smooth ride without the potential punctures of pneumatic tyres.

Even with an all-terrain pram, you should avoid walking across very rough ground with your young baby as he won't cope well with the jolting. A supportive sling or carrier is a better way to transport a newborn in such scenarios.

Urban streets

For city slickers, good manoeuvrability and swivel (rather than fixed) wheels will be crucial. Narrower prams are easier to get through shop doorways and aisles. Fixed-wheel three-wheelers can be especially problematic around towns but plenty of pushchairs are well suited to cities so you'll have a wide choice.

Rough Ground
££ Out'n'About Nipper Single

£££ Mountain Buggy

Urban Dwellers
££ Baby Jogger City Mini

£ Petite Star Zia, Petite Star Bubble (lightweight but with a reversible seat) • ££ Graco Evo (even lighter, reversible seat and carrycot option), Britax B-Agile, Bugaboo Bee, Mamas & Papas Sola, Babystyle Oyster, iCandy Cherry • £££ Bugaboo Cameleon, Uppababy Vista, Joolz Day
From six months:
£/££ Quinny Zapp or Yezz

How you'll travel

On foot

✳ **For Walking Everywhere**
£££ Uppababy Vista, Joolz Day, Bugaboo Cameleon · £££+ Orbit Baby (has unusual 360° rotating seat)

If you walk a lot, you might prefer a reversible seat unit so your baby can face you or look outwards. Research suggests having a baby facing his carer in the pushchair helps language development and bonding. A good suspension and larger wheels will ensure a comfier ride.

A generous shopping basket will be useful if you regularly shop on foot (Joolz Day has an extra large shopping bag, which is sold separately). Larger prams tend to have bigger baskets than lightweight buggies. Some models tip easily if you put heavy shopping on the handlebars but 'buggy weights' (see page 123) can help prevent this.

By car

✳ **For Small Boots**
£ Petite Star Zia · ££ Baby Jogger City Mini, Quinny Zapp Xtra, Britax B-Agile

Obviously, your chosen pushchair has to fit in your boot (measure up carefully) and leave space for other things, too, if you are using it on holiday or for an overnight trip.

Check the pushchair is easy to lift; getting a heavy pram in and out of your boot can literally be a pain, especially if you've had a caesarean. It's not just a question of comparing weights on paper – one 8 kg pram can feel a lot heavier than another depending on the way it folds and, consequently, the way you have to lift it.

Finally, think about how easily it folds and unfolds as you'll do this frequently if you use the car a lot. Some prams fold in one piece, others only once you remove the seat unit or carrycot. 'Two-piecers' are more fiddly but the weight is split so each piece is lighter. Avoid very heavy, bulky models as they can be annoying to get into the boot and take up a lot of space.

By bus and train

✳ **For Buses and Trains**
£ Petite Star Bubble · ££ BabyJogger City Mini, Britax B-Agile

Many buses now accommodate pushchairs without them having to be folded but do check out the routes you'll use. If you travel by bus or train a lot and need to collapse the pushchair, a one-hand fold will be crucial. Try a few as some supposedly one-hand-fold buggies definitely need two hands despite what the manufacturers say. A true, genuinely one-hand fold and open 'suitable from birth' model is the Baby

Jogger City Mini. The Britax B-Agile follows as a close second –
still a one-hand fold but with two actions to do it. Both can be
used from birth without the optional carrycot, but if a carrycot
is used, it must be removed before you can fold up the
pushchair.

Another option for public transport might be to use a sling
or carrier, particularly until your baby is old enough for a
lighter one-hand-fold buggy.

By plane

If you'll be flying a lot, choose something that folds easily, can
tackle sand or rough ground (depending on your destinations)
and is light. Many parents invest in lightweight small-wheeled
buggies for travel only to struggle over beaches or uneven
paths. If this will be problematic, go for a model with bigger
wheels such as the Micralite or Baby Jogger, and remember that
a sling or carrier can be immensely useful for such occasions.

If you might have another baby soon

If you're planning on a second baby relatively soon, it's worth
looking at 'convertible' pushchairs, which start as singles and
can be transformed into doubles (and back again once your
older child is walking everywhere). These are highly flexible,

✳ Plane Trips
*For city holidays post 6
months: ££* Quinny Zapp
and Yezz, most Maclarens
(some are suitable from
birth) • *For beach/rural
holidays: £* Chicco Echo •
££ Micralite Superlite,
BabyJogger City Mini

- -

PRODUCT SHOWCASE

Quinny produce two ultra-light pushchairs, the **Zapp** and **Yezz**, which are ideal for babies
over six months for frequent travel and occasional town use. The more established Zapp
folds up to a tiny 69 x 27 x 30 cm and weighs only 6 kg. Although very easy to push on
city streets, the smaller rubber wheels don't cope well with sand or uneven surfaces and
the seat unit isn't suitable for newborns (although you can use a Maxi-Cosi infant car
seat on it). The Yezz folds even tinier and is a kilo lighter; it's the lightest pushchair we're
aware of. It can also easily be slung over your shoulder when folded, should your toddler
want to walk. The seat doesn't recline and with this one there's no car seat option, so it's
only suitable from six months. Even for older babies and toddlers though, it probably
won't be comfy enough for day-long use or sleeping in and there's very limited storage
space. Still, it's a great holiday or second buggy.

- -

Another Baby
£££+ Bugaboo Donkey

££ BabyJogger City
Select • ££/£££ Phil&
Teds Inline models • £££
Mountain Buggy Plus
One, iCandy Peach

Twin Pushchair
££ Out'n'About Nipper
Double

£ OBaby Apollo •
££ Cosatto YouTwo
(cheerful bright designs),
BabyJogger City Mini
Twin (excellent all-
rounder) • £££ iCandy
Peach (head-turning
looks and practical, too),
Mountain Buggy Urban
Jungle Duo or Duet
(pricey but very
comfortable) • £££+
Bugaboo Donkey

although they are bigger and heavier than most single models. The originator of the single-to-double convertible concept was the Phil&Teds brand, with their so-called 'inline' models. Their success has since spawned the launch of many such pushchairs from other brands.

The original convertibles featured one seat at the back, which was suitable from birth, and another in front, which did not recline enough for a newborn. This meant they were only suitable for baby and toddler siblings or two toddlers, rather than newborn twins.

Some of the newer models build on the concept and offer more functionality – the option to add one or two car seats to form a travel system, one or two carrycots, and/or have two suitable-from-birth seats. This means they work for any combination of two siblings – two newborns, two toddlers or a toddler plus a newborn.

Note that although prospective buyers sometimes worry that the second seat on convertibles can be too close to the ground, in our experience, few owners report this as a problem.

There is also a side-by-side convertible – the Bugaboo Donkey. It's eye-wateringly expensive (from around £900 to £1,200 depending on the configuration you buy but extremely versatile with the option to have pushchair seats facing in or out, one or two carrycots or one or two car seats.

If you're having twins

For twins, your first decision is between a 'tandem' (one child sits behind the other) and a 'side-by-side' model.

Overall, we prefer side-by-sides for twins, provided they fit through normal doorways (not all do, so check before buying). However, if you decide on a tandem, ideally choose one where the rear seat is elevated enough for the second baby to see out. Also, beware of very long models, which can make crossing roads feel perilous because the front of the pram will be so far ahead of you.

A few twin pushchairs have optional carrycots – either two singles or a double shared by both babies. Generally, single carrycots are easier to handle if you anticipate detaching the carrycot quite often.

TANDEMS OR SIDE-BY-SIDE FOR TWINS?

	Tandem	Side-by-side
Manoeuvrability	Can be very long, making crossing roads problematic; getting through doorways/shop aisles easy	Width can make even standard doorways and shop aisles tricky.
Can the babies interact with each other?	Not easily	Yes
Do both seats recline?	Depends on model	Yes on most models
Can they both see out?	Visibility will be limited for the rear child unless the seat is elevated	Both get a decent view

Look for pneumatic wheels, which usually go hand in hand with decent suspension for twin prams as these make pushing two toddlers (which your newborns will eventually be) easier.

If you want to jog with your baby
If jogging with your baby appeals, you'll need a lightweight, fixed-wheel three-wheeler, preferably with a handlebar-mounted brake lever for increased control on hills and rear wheels of 16 inches or more for a smoother ride.

Unless a fixed-wheel three-wheeler would suit the rest of your lifestyle (you live in the country), we suggest waiting until your baby reaches six months as you'll have more choice, including some cheaper models that are only suitable after that age.

All-rounders
If no single issue is critical for you, our 'all-rounders' make solid choices: they're a great bet in most scenarios and should take you through the whole period from birth until your pram-pushing days are over. The Baby Jogger City Mini is hard to beat for all-round value while the Uppababy Vista, although more expensive, has more functionality e.g. a reversible seat.

For family outings and holidays it might be worth investing in two cheap single buggies so when you and your partner are together, you can take one twin each. Choose the same type of buggy and you can buy a connector (Prince Lionheart do some) to fit them together when one of you is on your own.

Jogging
££ Out'n'About Nipper Sport, **Baby Jogger Summit XC**, **Baby Jogger Performance** (for serious joggers) • £££ **Mountain Buggy Terrain**

All-rounder
££ Baby Jogger City Mini
• £££ UppaBaby Vista

££ Britax B-Agile,
Mamas&Papas Sola •
£££ ICandy Cherry •
£££+ Joolz Day

If you think you could manage solely with a sling or carrier for the first few months, you could skip the carrycot/lie-flat phase, and buy only a cheaper, lightweight buggy later on. A reclining seat will still be important if you want your baby to nap in the buggy but it needn't lie completely flat once your baby is older.

The Joolz Day is a wonderful luxury option.

For most people, something with a detachable carrycot, that later converts to a lightweight, easy-to-fold buggy, will offer the best value and reduce the chance of you needing a different push chair later on.

Look for...
Essential

* *An adjustable or appropriate height handle* This is especially important if you and your partner or other regular carers are of very different heights and one of you is particularly short or tall.

* *Decent brakes* Look for brakes on both wheels, not just one.

* *Manoeuvrability* A lighter-weight pram might be easier to lift in and out of the car than a heavy one but won't necessarily be easier to push. Swivel wheels that can also be fixed in position are beneficial because you can adjust them to suit different terrain. Suspension and wheel type affect manoeuvrability, too. Check whether you can push the pushchair one-handed as this can be useful; bar handles are good for this.

* *A comfortable-looking seat*, ideally in a breathable fabric to prevent your baby getting clammy in hot weather; adding a sheepskin liner can help with this.

* *A smooth, easy-to-use recline mechanism* Some models jolt your baby awake when you are trying to recline the pushchair or can be fiddly.

* *Foam-covered or soft plastic handles* These are more comfortable than hard plastic.

* *Light and easy to fold.*

* *Adjustable, padded harness.*

* *Car seat compatibility* As we've already said, sitting in a car seat for too long isn't good for your baby but a travel system option can by handy. Be careful when choosing one, however, as the car seat that comes with a particular travel system might not fit in your car or might not perform well in crash tests.

Useful

❋ *A reversible seat* allows your baby to face you, encouraging interaction, or to face out so he can see the world better.

❋ *Pneumatic or foam-filled wheels* make for a smoother ride for your baby and easier pushing for you. Pneumatic wheels can puncture and will need pumping up from time to time (lining the inner wheel with Slime sealant will help prevent punctures).

❋ *A generous basket* will be useful for carrying the incredible amount of stuff that you need for a baby and into which you may even manage to fit some shopping! Check accessibility when the pushchair seat is reclined.

❋ *A decently sized hood* Some pushchair hoods are too small to be effective, others are extendable or can offer sun protection. If the model you like doesn't have a large enough sun hood, you might need to add a sun protection cover (see page 122). Some larger hoods have clear 'viewing windows', which are useful but really not essential.

If you aren't shy, a great way to get the lowdown on a pram you're considering, is to approach people in the street who are pushing one and asking them if they're happy with it.

Don't worry about...

❋ *Accessories* Although rain covers, footmuffs, umbrellas and insect nets contribute to the 'real' price of the pushchair, most extras can be bought separately and some are unnecessary (see below).

❋ *Bumper bars* Some toddlers like holding on to these but, unless they swing open to the side, they can get in the way when lifting your child in and out.

PUSHCHAIR ACCESSORIES

Some pushchair purchase prices include co-ordinating accessories; others are charged for separately and may be expensive. Generic alternatives are often cheaper and may perform as well, if not better than branded ones.

Sunshade
Outlook Shade-a-babe,
Snoozeshade (universal
UV shades)

SUN PROTECTION

Carrycots come with a hood and apron, which will offer good protection. All but the cheapest buggies have integral canopies or hoods but these vary in their effectiveness. The best are extendable to cover more of your child.

Parasols are pretty ineffective unless you stay in a fixed spot; when you walk, the directon of sunlight alters all the time. A sun shade that fits over the whole buggy is much better and some pushchair manufacturers now offer these as part of their co-ordinated range.

RAIN COVERS

Most buggies and carrycots come with rain covers. You can buy generic ones separately from nursery stores but these might not fit quite as well as the ones specifically designed for a particular pushchair.

FOOTMUFFS/COSYTOES

These are like little outdoor sleeping bags for use on the pushchair. They aren't essential but help keep your baby cosy in colder weather. Unlike blankets, a footmuff cannot fall (or be kicked) off the buggy into a muddy puddle. Note, footmuffs aren't needed for carrycots as these provide better weather protection than buggies and you can use pram blankets without them falling off. Choose a footmuff./cosytoes with a zip-off front/top for easy removal and access to your baby. This type can double as a buggy liner in summer.

Sheepskin-lined versions are more breathable than those with a synthetic lining and help regulate temperature.

Generic footmuffs can be bought from nursery stores and are often cheaper than branded ones from a particular pushchair range. It won't be the end of the world if it doesn't match the buggy fabric exactly but do check it will fit the seat and harness properly.

A footmuff with a double zip will usually last longer, as even for a taller toddler, you can undo the bottom end only, and let his feet stick out, but still keep his legs and body warm.

SHEEPSKIN LINERS

These keep babies cooler in summer and warmer in winter, have properties that are believed to calm and soothe babies and are a great way to make a flimsy, lightweight buggy seat

more comfortable. However, their bulk can make it hard to fold umbrella buggies, so bear this in mind. Check for pre-cut holes for the buggy's harness to feed through and that the liner is machine washable.

TRAVEL BAGS

A durable, waterproof bag can provide protection from wear and tear but generally is only worthwhile if you'll frequently travel by plane and have to stow the pushchair in the hold. However, countless prams do get damaged in transit so buying one can ultimately save you money and aggravation.

You should wait and see if you need one, depending on your travel plans. You could always share the cost of buying one with a friend, if you can be fairly confident your holidays won't clash.

PRAM TOYS

These are a welcome way to keep babies occupied when shopping. Their advantage over ordinary toys is they clip on and therefore can't be dropped or lobbed off (there is truth in that old phrase about 'throwing your toys out of the pram').

✳ **Pram Toys**
Baby Whoozit Spiral, Tiny Love Take Along Arch

✳ **Buggybooks, Bondie Bird Playwrap** (can be used off the pushchair, too), **Heimess Wooden Pram Clip and String**

BUGGY WEIGHTS

If your pushchair is tippy (and some are, especially if you hang shopping over the handles), you can add cheap buggy weights to the front wheels to rebalance it. Weights don't adversely affect manoeuvrability.

●→ *A buggy board (also known as a 'surfer' or 'ride-on' board) fixes on the back of your pushchair and creates a small platform for a toddler or pre-schooler to stand on and hitch a ride. They're a popular option for parents if their child gets tired walking on occasion or walks slowly, which can be troublesome when you're in a hurry. Boards also 'bridge the gap' for some parents whose older child is almost ready to walk full time when their new baby arrives, letting them skip buying a double buggy (which is an extra expense and more cumbersome than a single). When choosing a buggy board, check it's compatible with your pushchair; ask the retailer for help with this. The original Buggy*

Board from Lascal has been copied but still remains the best option in our view and fits on most pushchairs. Some pushchair brands offer proprietary boards, which can be useful as you can be sure of a good fit but if you'll change your pushchair at some stage, you may not then be able to use it on the new one.

SLINGS AND CARRIERS

Slings and carriers have a slightly hippy image in some people's eyes but we're huge fans and so are legions of other parents who've found that 'wearing' their baby is good for them and for their little one.

Baby wearing comes into its own on countless occasions, from the everyday – freeing hands for housework if your baby doesn't like being put down, 'buggy-free' shopping trips or jumping on a bus without dragging a folded pram – to rarer times, such as ambling across countryside, with which even the most rugged of all-terrain prams can't cope, or at the airport if your buggy has had to go in the hold. Most importantly, the majority of babies love being carried this way.

The terms 'slings' and 'carriers' are used pretty inter-changeably but strictly speaking, slings are less structured and hammock-like, whereas carriers have more buckles and straps and a padded 'seat' for the baby to sit in, usually in an upright position.

REASONS TO LOVE BABY WEARING
Benefits for babies
* Being carried in a sling/carrier is comforting, like an extension of the womb. It promotes bonding and is especially positive for babies with colic or reflux.
* Babies view and interact with the world from a higher vantage point and are more 'included' in conversations than they can be in a pram.

Benefits for you
* The closeness to your baby can be heart-warming (and literally body-warming – lovely when it's chilly although less so on a scorching day).

- If your baby is the type who screams when you put him down or needs rocking to sleep, your hands are free to tackle the million tasks involved in being a new parent.
- You can leave the pushchair behind!
- Slings and carriers are practical on occasions when a pushchair can be a liability, such as during country walks, in crowded places and on public transport. When shopping, you can skip the lift and get through aisles/doors/up escalators more easily than with a pushchair.
- Some slings and carriers allow for discreet breastfeeding – ideal if you feel shy about 'public exposure'.
- If you also have a toddler still needing a pushchair, you can put your newborn in a sling or carrier to bridge the gap until the older one can walk all the time or use a buggy board. This might allow you to avoid buying the dreaded double buggy, which might only be needed for a few months.

If at first you don't succeed...

If slings and carriers are so indispensible, how come most of us know people who bought one, tried it and gave up? The problem is that the first few times you use obe, you're working with something unfamiliar while holding a wriggly, wobbly-headed newborn at the same time. Using a carrier takes practice and it can be intimidating to get your baby in and out of one initially, especially if you're worried about upsetting, or worse dropping, your baby as you sort out a tangle of buckles and straps.

So choose a model that's easy to use and persevere. If a friend has the same one, ask her to show you how to use it. If not, ask someone at the shop to do a demo or at least get someone else to help the first few times. If the instruction leaflet is confusing, check the internet for video demos. Practising with a doll might feel silly but could help. Your efforts will be rewarded, we promise.

So can I do without a pram then?

We know a couple of parents who carried their children in slings and managed without a pram, but most people use slings in addition to a pram. Certainly, if baby carrying really

Assuming there aren't always two adults around, there are still options when it comes to 'wearing' twins. You could use a single wrap or ring/shoulder sling (see page 129) to hold two young babies or you could wear two slings, one for each baby. There are also a few specialist 'double' carriers about, such as The Weego (try www.TwinsUK.co.uk). Obviously, carrying two babies at once will be more of a strain so you might not manage to do it for long.

Slings and carriers lend themselves well to secondhand purchase. Most are washable so won't seem much different if they're 'pre-loved'.

appeals, it's quite realistic to use only a sling or carrier for the first months, dodging the lie-flat pram stage. Once your baby gets too heavy to carry around so much, she'll be old enough for a lighter-weight, cheaper buggy.

Overall though, we recommend slings and carriers as a complement to a pram. Sometimes a pram is genuinely easier; eating and drinking with a baby in a front carrier can be tricky, for example. You could try managing with just the carrier and see how you get on.

Where to buy?

Most nursery retailers carry only a limited range. For more choice, try online sling specialists such as Little Possums, Bigmamaslings or The Carrying Kind; these guys live and breathe slings and carriers and will work with you to find one to suit your needs. Some specialists offer hire services, so you can see if you get on with a particular brand before buying.

Front or back? In or out?

In the beginning, you'll need to carry your baby on your front, usually facing in until he can support his own head, and then outwards later on.

Until what age you manage to carry your baby on your front before your back and shoulders hurt depends on which model you have, your own strength and stature and whether your baby is a bruiser or a tiddler. Typically we find mums can use a front carrier until their baby is around six months old before stopping or switching to a back carrier (see page 179); dads usually manage for a little longer.

Sling types that distribute a baby's weight well can give you up to 18 months of carrying in front and a few, including the Ergo and Manduca carriers (see Product Showcase), can be used on both the front and back.

TYPES OF SLINGS/CARRIER

STRUCTURED CARRIERS

These carriers (the best known is the BabyBjörn) hold your baby next to your chest in an upright position. They usually have a padded section for the baby to sit in and adjustable straps and buckles to position the carrier correctly. A padded flap provides support for your newborn's floppy head when he faces inwards and this flap is then folded down when your baby moves to the forward-facing position once he can support his own head.

+ Can feel more secure than slings and for many people are easier to use.
+ Good for windy babies as there's slight pressure on the digestive system. Babies with reflux also benefit from the upright rather than more horizontal position of most slings.
+ Adjustable to fit different-sized wearers.
- Fewer carrying positions than some slings.
- Not as suited to breastfeeding as some slings.
- There are concerns (although there's no firm evidence) that some carriers provide inadequate support in this upright position, which can result in too much pressure bearing down from the head on to a baby's spine.
- Some have a minimum weight of 3.5 kilos (8 lbs) or more – although this isn't an issue for long unless you have a small or premature baby.

Structured Carrier
BabyBjörn (for ease of use), Manduca or Ergo (for weight distribution and longevity)

PRODUCT SHOWCASE

The **Ergo** and **Manduca** are similar products, which stand out among more structured carriers because each can be worn comfortably on either your front or back and therefore can be used from birth (with the optional newborn insert in the Ergo's case; this is integral on the Manduca) right through the toddler years. Older babies and toddlers love the back carrying position, which is rather like a supported piggyback, and younger babies are in a more supportive, less upright position than with other carriers. The smart-looking Stokke MyCarrier also offers front and back positions but the straps aren't as well-padded, making carrying a heavier toddler less comfortable, and it's more expensive.

Verdict: This is a matter of personal choice; some parents prefer the look of structured carriers and find slings too 'hippyish'. If you're unlikely to persevere with instructions, a carrier might suit you better than a sling.

WRAP SLINGS

Wrap Sling
££ Close Parent Caboo
DX (user-friendly) • £££
Hug-a-Bub

Fundamentally these are long pieces of fabric that wrap around wearer and baby, securing baby in place. They're highly supportive for newborns and suitable from a lower birth weight than most structured carriers and easy to breastfeed in. They also distribute weight more evenly across your whole torso. But they can be quite daunting to use at first, so aren't ideal if you aren't the persevering type.

Some wraps are made from stretchy T-shirt type material, others from woven cotton. The former are lovely and cosseting but some stretch too much to support a heavier, older baby.

+ Several carrying positions – including sometimes on your back – mean some of these slings can be used until your baby is 18 to 24 months old.
+ They work well for carrying premature babies as they are so supportive.
+ One size usually fits all for stretchy wraps (woven wraps tend to come in different sizes).

PRODUCT SHOWCASE

The **Wilkinet** and **Close DX** are a cross between a carrier and a wrap sling with slightly more structure and plenty of padding for comfort. They are a great middle ground between a BabyBjorn type carrier and a standard wrap and have several carrying positions. With the Wilkinet a drawback is that you have to sit down to put it on, which isn't always practical.

+ Their upright carrying positions are great for babies with reflux or colic and the hammock position is well-suited to breastfeeding.

+ Easy to wash and dry, and pack reasonably small.

- Tricky to master at first; you'll need to persevere.

Verdict: Our favourite type of sling but steer clear if you give up easily on things! Among traditional wraps we prefer stretchy fabric to woven, although they might not work for quite so long with heavy toddlers.

RING SLINGS

Also known as shoulder or bag carriers, ring slings are lengths of fabric threaded through two attached rings, enabling easy adjustment. Some have a padded section to provide extra comfort for a baby – especially nice for a newborn – but this can limit how adjustable the sling will be, which can be a problem if you and your partner are very different sizes. Padding also means the sling will take up more space in your bag (although they're still very compact) and could be too warm in mid-summer.

Ring Sling
££ Maya

   The BabaSling is similar in design to standard ring slings but has an easy-adjust buckle rather than rings and a padded shoulder, which stops the fabric digging into you, making it more comfortable.

+ Adjustability means both partners can use the same sling.

+ Well-suited to breastfeeding.

+ Non-padded ring slings pack small.

Pouch Sling
££ The Tricotti, Hotslings
(amongst more traditional
pouches)

- Can take some getting used to at first (although after the initial period they are easy to use). It's particularly important to ensure this type of sling is used correctly for newborns, to avoid any suffocation risk because of the way your baby lies inside the fabric. See page 132 for safe use advice.
- Not ideal for an older baby if you have a bad back.

Verdict: We aren't big fans of the standard ring slings but some people swear by them. Slings that are padded only in the shoulder, like the Maya, offer a good compromise between comfort and adjustability.

POUCH SLINGS

These are simple tubes or sashes of fabric worn over one shoulder – not dissimilar to a sling for broken arms. They're very easy to use with no confusing buckles or straps; you just put your baby in the little pouch of fabric and go. They're a good choice if you'll take your baby in and out a lot. The big downside is that these slings come in quite specific sizes and the wrong size will not be comfortable for you, secure for your baby or fit differently sized wearers.

+ Very easy to use.
+ Compact – can be shoved in a bag.
+ Hold newborns in a 'natural' reclined position akin to cradling a baby in your arms.
+ Several different carrying positions, so work well for both newborns and toddlers (the latter for short periods only).
- Not adjustable.

PRODUCT SHOWCASE

Unlike most pouches, the **Tricotti** has two pieces of fabric rather than one, so it goes over both shoulders and weight is distributed much more evenly so the pouch can be used for older babies and toddlers. It's also hugely practical as it packs away so small. The Tricotti won't fit very petite or large wearers, though, and you'll need to be careful to buy the right size for your baby.

- Weight is concentrated on one shoulder (with the exception of the Tricotti), so is not distributed evenly – a problem for longer use with heavier babies and toddlers.

Verdict: If a pouch appeals, the Tricotti is hard to beat.

Look for...
Whichever type of sling or carrier appeals, there are several features to consider.
Essential
❋ *Ease of use* If it's not easy to get on and get your baby into, you'll be less likely to use it.
❋ *Washability* Most, but not all, are machine washable.
❋ *Comfort and security for your baby* A good sling will be both comfortable and supportive for your baby, so you can move around without feeling the need to keep a hand on her.
❋ *Comfort for you* This is especially important if you want to continue to use a carrier or sling as your baby gets heavier or if you have a bad back. Choose something that distributes weight evenly. One that concentrates weight on your upper back and shoulders or is one-sided will be hard to use once your baby is heavier. Look for wide straps and adjustability.

Useful
❋ *Longevity* If you want to use one sling or carrier through to the toddler years, look at the recommended weight range and choose one with several different carrying positions. Newborns are best carried on your front facing in or in a horizontal fetal-like position; older babies and toddlers will want to face outwards so they have something to look at. Models that carry a toddler on your hip or back are better for later on.
❋ *Unisex fabric and fit* If both you and your partner will use the sling, you might want to avoid anything flowery or girly. Most slings and carriers adjust to fit a range of builds but a few, especially pouch slings, come in specific sizes and will not fit people of different builds.
❋ *A breastfeeding 'position'* This allows you to breastfeed your baby in the sling or carrier; doing so takes some getting used

"It is possible to manage without a pram. I love carrying my daughter around – she's now 11 months. We've literally only ever used a pram once; we borrowed one for a wedding so she had somewhere to nap."

to but can provide discretion for mums who don't want to reveal all to the wider world. Ring slings, wrap slings and some pouch slings are especially suited to this.

❋ *Packs small* A sling or carrier that you can shove in a bag when not using it is a good idea.

❋ *Accessories* Babies in slings and carriers can be exposed to the elements; some models have a rain hood or sun shade or a fleecy winter cover. These can be worthwhile but you can manage without (your hands will be free for an umbrella and it isn't worth choosing a particular brand on this basis). Some carriers such as the BabyBjörn offer dribble bibs, which stop the carrier getting soaked with drool but draping a muslin cloth over the carrier will also do the job.

SLING SAFETY

It's important to ensure you use a baby sling or carrier correctly, following the manufacturer's instructions. There could be a suffocation risk.

These guidelines are from the Baby Sling Safe Campaign, and are five simple points to always keep in mind when 'slinging' your little one. They apply to newborns up to four month olds particularly. The campaign is really easy to remember thanks to the acronym **T.I.C.K.S.**

❋ **TIGHT**
The sling should hold your passenger tightly but gently against you.

❋ **IN VIEW**
You must always be able to see your baby's face; it must never be covered or in danger of being covered by any fabric.

❋ **CLOSE TO KISS**
When being carried in the sling it is important that your child is close enough to kiss; you should be able to bend down and kiss her at any time.

❋ **KEEP CHIN UP**
When riding in a sling, a baby's head should never slouch down so her chin is forced against her chest, this can be dangerous and makes it difficult to breathe.

❋ **SUPPORT**
A baby's back should be supported in a natural way, as if you were cradling her. You can check this by gently pushing on your baby's back; she should not move.

CAR SEATS AND DRIVING ACCESSORIES

BUYING A CAR SEAT

In order to drive your baby home from hospital, you will need to have a car seat fitted. While choosing one might be slightly dull compared to other aspects of baby shopping, an infant car seat is one of the most important and safety-conscious baby-related purchases you'll make, so it really is worth investing enough time to do it properly. And we don't just mean selecting one in a colour to match your car's upholstery.

All seats sold new in the UK reach minimum safety standards but some go beyond what is 'required' and perform better than others in crash tests. All our recommended brands do very well in these tests.

SHOPPING LIST

- ✓ Group 0+ 'infant carrier' car seat
- ? Car seat base
- ? Car seat footmuff
- ? Sun blinds
- ? Special mirror so you can see your baby in a rear-facing seat
- ✗ 'Baby on Board' sign

When possible, infants shouldn't sit in car seats for more than two hours at a time, and, ideally, for a maximum of two hours per day. Research shows newborns can develop breathing problems when they spend long periods hunched in car seats and there are worries about the long-term effect on spinal development. If you're going on a long car journey, have a break every couple of hours, taking your baby out of his seat so she can stretch and lie flat for a while. Bear this in mind if you're considering buying a travel system pushchair (see page 112); it shouldn't be used for long periods in car seat mode.

Once you've bought your seat, practise fitting it in the car before your baby's due date; taking your baby home can be intimidating enough without having to faff around with car seat fitting instructions, while your newborn screams the car park down.

For second-stage car seats (suitable from 9 kg) see page 181.

CAR SEAT GOLDEN RULES
A car seat MUST:

✷ *Fit the car or cars it will be used in* Not all seats fit all cars. Before buying one, check its suitability for your make and model of car – this applies to both ISOFIX and non-ISOFIX seats (see box on the opposite page). Consult the manufacturer's website or call its customer care line (or get the retailer to do so) for the most up-to-date list of compatible cars. Alternatively, with non-ISOFIX, 'belted' seats, a reputable retailer can do an on-the-spot check for fit in your car. With ISOFIX models, it's essential to consult the manufacturer's official list of approved vehicles as seats can appear to fit but there can be unseen problems.

✷ *Be the right size for your child's weight (not her age)* Age isn't as relevant as weight when it comes to car seat safety.

✷ *Be bought new* unless you know for sure the seat has not been in an accident, is less than five years old and the manual is available. Only use a secondhand seat if you know it hasn't been in an accident as no matter how minor, this

CAR SEAT GROUPS

	Faces	Weight range	Approx. age range
Group 0	rear	birth to 10 kg	birth to approx. 9 months
Group 0+	rear	birth to 13 kg	birth to approx. 15 months
Group 1	forward	9 kg to 18 kg	9 months to approx. 4 years
Group 2/3	forward	15 kg to 36 kg	3 years to 12 years

ABOUT ISOFIX

You'll see the term **ISOFIX** (International Standards Organisation FIX) a lot when car seat shopping. Whereas 'standard' car seats secure using an adult seat belt, ISOFIX ones plug into two fixing points at the rear of the backseat, attaching rigidly to the car chassis. In the case of infant carriers, this will be via a base that is semi-permanently fixed in the car; you simply clip the carrier on and off the base.

As well as the two rear seat latches, some ISOFIX systems use a third fixing point called a top tether (but not all cars have these), or have a rigid support leg to enhance stability.

Since 2006, ISOFIX fittings have been compulsory in all new cars but some earlier models have them too. Feel between the rear seat back and base for the fixings (or get a car seat retailer to look for you), check the manual, or ask the car dealer, if you bought the car from an official dealership.

Be aware that just because your car has ISOFIX fixings, it doesn't mean that all ISOFIX seats will fit; you'll still need to check the compatibility of a particular model for your car.

could compromise its safety in a subsequent collision. Car seat design improves all the time and newer models are likely to be safer than those produced more than a few years ago. Additionally, polystyrene, the main shock-absorbing component in infant carriers, degrades over time so might not perform as well on a seat that's over five years old, as when new. For these reasons, we thoroughly recommend buying a new seat whenever possible.

❋ *Be installed properly* Even the best performers in crash tests won't be safe if they aren't fitted correctly. No matter how simple installation is, if you don't take care to read the instructions, it's easy to get it wrong; surveys suggest between 50 and 75% of car seats are incorrectly fitted. Most nursery stores will have someone knowledgeable do a demo in your car then watch you doing it, although some charge a small fee this service, refundable on purchase of a seat. Some manufacturers' websites have helpful video instructions on fitting their car seats. Most ISOFIX seats have an indicator to confirm correct fitting, which can be

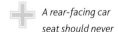 *A rear-facing car seat should never be used on a front passenger seat with an active airbag. The safest place for a rear-facing seat is in the middle of the back seat. You can sometimes de-activate airbags but even then, siting an infant car seat on the front seat should be a last resort; the back is always safer.*

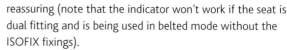

✷ **ISOFIX Car Seat**
££ Maxi-Cosi CabrioFix •
£££ Maxi-Cosi Pebble
(with either EasyFix or
FamilyFix Bases)

✷ ££ Britax Baby-Safe
and Baby-Safe Plus SHR
II, Recaro Young Profi Plus
• £££ BeSafe iZi Sleep
(lies flat)

reassuring (note that the indicator won't work if the seat is dual fitting and is being used in belted mode without the ISOFIX fixings).

✷ *Have a correctly fitting harness* You should check the harness every journey and adjust it to fit your baby, depending on the thickness of her clothing. It should fit snug to her body; too many layers of thick clothing can reduce its safety in the event of a collision. Remember, too, to adjust the height of the harness from time to time as your baby grows. The top of the harness straps should always be sitting at or slightly below her shoulder level.

Is it worth paying extra for ISOFIX?

The most recent crash tests suggest that ISOFIX seats with either a rigid support leg or top tether (a third, upper anchorage point for extra stability) are the safest option and certainly perform better than seats fitted using an adult seat belt. Additionally, ISOFIX significantly reduces the possibility of incorrect fitting, a very common problem that compromises safety. One study showed that only 30% of 'belted' seats were fitted correctly, whereas 96% of ISOFIX ones were. Certainly, if your car has the fixings, the extra peace of mind probably makes it worth paying more for an ISOFIX seat and base.

ISOFIX infant carriers can also be used in non-ISOFIX cars, secured by the regular seat belt. In this scenario, they are usually fitted without the base, although some ISOFIX bases are dual-fitting so can be 'belted' in place with the adult seat belt. Because ISOFIX child seats are more expensive than standard versions (an additional £100 or so for the base), it doesn't make sense to buy one if your main car doesn't have the fixings.

Seats with non-ISOFIX bases

A few manufacturers (notably Maxi-Cosi, Graco, Mamas & Papas and Chicco) offer non-ISOFIX bases for as little as £30 extra. As with ISOFIX infant carrier systems, the base stays in the car (in this instance, secured by the seat belt) and the seat clicks on. With some models, you do also have to stretch the seat belt round the back of the seat to secure it each time you

put the seat into the car. You should also check that your non-ISOFIX base is firmly fitted from time to time as it can loosen.

Crucially, although these bases make putting the car seat in the car easier, they don't provide the additional safety benefits of ISOFIX. Note that each manufacturer's base will only work with its corresponding car seats, so you cannot, say, use a Maxi-Cosi base with a Graco car seat.

Verdict: Potentially worthwhile if your car doesn't have ISOFIX and you want the convenience of just clicking the car seat on to a base.

Look for...
Essential

❉ *Compatibility with your car* See golden rules, page 134.
❉ *Portability* Carrying your baby around in her car seat while out of the car can be convenient and also provides somewhere for her to sit (for short periods only; see safety advice on page 134). A Group 0/0+ seat is the only type that allows this as it has handles and is usually quite compact – hence the term 'infant carrier'. Some models are more cumbersome than others. Look for a lightweight seat and a comfortable handle, and avoid anything that seems awkward to carry.
❉ *Soft, easily removable and washable covers.*
❉ *A head hugger* This is a cushion that fits around a newborn's head and provides extra support. It is important in that initial, wobbly-headed stage, preventing lolling about. (These can be bought separately, if needed.)
❉ *Chest and buckle pads* These are padded covers that prevent the buckle and straps digging into your baby. All but the most basic models have them.

Useful

❉ *ISOFIX (see above)* or a seat with a non-ISOFIX base (if your car doesn't have ISOFIX).
❉ *Spare 'summer' covers* These stop the seat getting clammy in summer and can be taken off easily for washing.
❉ *Compatibility with a pram chassis/travel system* Many

Non-ISOFIX Car Seat
£ Cosatto, Kiddy Nest • ££ Britax Baby Safe • £££ Maxi-Cosi Pebble or Cabriofix (without the base), BeSafe IZi Sleep (lie-flat)

parents like to whisk their car seat out of the car straight on to a pram chassis. Using one of these 'travel systems' means you're less likely to disturb your baby if she has nodded off in the car. This is indeed convenient but, as we've said, infants should only be in upright car seats for short periods. Choosing a seat that can also lie flat on the pram overcomes this but they have some drawbacks, too (see below).

Lie-flat Car Seat
£££ BeSafe IZi Sleep

❊ *Lie-flat capability* A few infant carriers lie flat. This overcomes worries about the poor positioning of babies in 'normal' car seats, and also means that your baby has a flat place to rest out of the car, without you having to take a carrycot or similar along (although such car seats cannot be used for overnight sleeping). There are two types: those that are flat both in the car and outside of it (for example, the Jane Transporter and Britax Baby-Safe Sleeper) and those that are upright in the car and only flat when out of it (the BeSafe IZi Sleep).

Car seats that lie flat all the time are similar to in-car carrycots. Traditionally these have not performed well in crash tests but two recent models, the Britax Baby-Safe Sleeper and Jane Transporter, have scored very well in independent safety testing. Both can make up a lie-flat travel system with compatible pushchairs from the same brands. Although officially Group 0 'seats', neither has an upright option so they are unlikely to be suited to babies above around six months. Both are therefore expensive choices, as you'll then have to go and buy a second seat to

cover the remaining months of the Group 0+ stage; six months is too young to transfer to a standard Group 1 seat (see below for information on combination Group 0+/ Group 1 seats, which would make most sense in this scenario). Other seemingly similar 'auto' carrycots are available but generally don't receive great press in terms of crash-test performance. The Britax and the Jane have enhanced safety features and are currently the only carrycot-style seats we're aware of that score as well as a regular Group 0+ car seat for safety.

If you are considering a car seat, which lies flat in the car and have older children, make sure there's enough space on the back seat for it and any other car seat(s).

Seats that you fit in an upright position in the car but are flat when taken out, such as the BeSafe Izi Sleep, are valuable if you want to use a travel system for longer periods. You should, however, steer clear of using any seat other than the Britax or Jane in lie-flat mode in a moving vehicle due to safety concerns.

Verdict: A lie-flat seat is practical if you want to use the seat for longer periods, either alone or on a pushchair chassis. Your pram choice will be limited to a compatible chassis. If you go for the Britax or the Jane, you need to consider the expense of having to buy a second Group 0+ car seat once it is outgrown (a combination Group 0/1 seat could be a solution).

- ❉ *A one-pull harness* Harnesses need adjusting every journey to ensure they remain snug according to the thickness of your baby's clothes. A 'one-pull' harness (straps are tightened with a single pull), makes this quicker and easier.
- ❉ *Rocking base* When using the car seat out of the car as a baby chair, a shaped base allows the seat to be rocked on the ground. This is a good way to soothe a fretful baby.
- ❉ *Sun canopy and rain cover* If you're going to carry your baby around in the car seat out of the car or on the pram, these are worthwhile. Sun canopies are often integral to first-stage seats but rain covers usually have to be bought separately.

Steer clear of...

* *Group 0+/1 combination seats* While these can be a money-saving option as a single seat does both the Group 0+ and Group 1 phases (from birth to around age four), generally, such combination seats are let down by the fact they are not as portable as standard Group 0+ infant carriers; they're too big and don't have a handle. This can be problematic as most parents find it useful to leave their baby in the seat for short periods. Additionally, surveys suggest these seats are the ones most likely to be fitted incorrectly as they're more complicated to attach to a car. Overall, in trying to be two products in one, we don't find they do either job quite as well as a seat for each phase would.

If you really want to go down this route, for fit and ease of use, the Concord Ultimax, the Britax First Class Plus, or the Maxi Cosi Opal are probably the best. Note that the BeSafe IZi Combi in our product showcase, below, is officially classified and approved as a Group 0+/Group 1 seat but the manufacturer only recommends it for use from six months and not from birth. This is because it recognises that although it passes standards, it will not perform as well as a dedicated Group 0+ seat for a child under six months.

* *Car seat footmuff* Unless you'll use the car seat on a pram chassis a lot, a blanket will do just fine and be cheaper and more versatile (but keep it over rather than under the harness). Most modern cars are pretty warm, so thick coverings are unnecessary.

Travel systems

Some car seats aren't compatible with any pushchairs, some are only sold as part of a 'travel system' and a few fit on several different pushchair chassis. With early travel systems, you always had to buy a particular brand's car seat and pushchair together but in recent years, many systems have become semi-universal. Maxi-Cosi's popular CabrioFix and Pebble seats can be fitted on to a wide range of pushchairs from other makers (including Bugaboo, Micralite, Mountain Buggy, Phil&Teds, iCandy, Stokke, Quinny, Uppababy and Joolz, among others), although you may need to buy adapters to do

this. BeSafe and Cybex (sold in Mamas & Papas) ensure that at least some of their Group 0+ seats can also be used on the same pushchairs as the Maxi-Cosi ones.

Do not be swayed, however, into buying a car seat that doesn't fit your car properly just because it goes on the pushchair you want; this could be dangerous.

Verdict: A travel system is a useful and popular option if you're swapping between car and pushchair a lot and don't want to disturb your baby. Bear in mind that only those with a lie-flat capability, once transferred to the pushchair wheels, should be used for longer than a couple of hours at a time.

Replace any child seat that has been in an accident – even minor impacts can affect the protection it will offer and any damage might not be apparent. Your insurance company will usually cover the cost of a new one.

Changing to a forward-facing seat

In Scandinavian countries, it's common for toddlers to use a rear-facing, Group 1 seat as opposed to a forward-facing one (the most commonly-used type in the UK). Research shows that even at this stage, rearward facing remains safer than forward facing. At the time of writing, we expect a change to UK law, probably in 2013, which will require babies to stay rearward facing until 15 months. Currently, many parents switch to forward facing earlier than this because the next stage, Group 1 seats have a minimum weight of 9 kg (20 lbs), and Group 0+ seats have a maximum weight of 13 kg (28 lb 9 oz). Even before any change in the law, bear in mind that it's best to keep your baby rear facing for as long as possible

- -

PRODUCT SHOWCASE

BeSafe IZi Combi is one of the only seats currently on the market in the UK in which your child can remain facing the rear until he reaches 18 kg (about four years of age). You do have the option of using it forward facing for the Group 1 stage and above, if you feel you or your child would prefer that at some point. Although classified as a Group 0+/1 model, this is best used from six months, rather than from birth, so it could be a good option to follow on from the Britax Safer Sleeper carrycot or bought after a normal Group 0+ seat is outgrown.

- -

"I always keep a bag in the car with spare nappies, wipes and a set of Joshua's clothes. It's great for unexpected situations or times when I've forgotten something - which happens all too often with 'baby brain'."

✳ Sun Blinds

Clippasafe, Diono, Safety 1st; Windowsox and Outlook Autoshades (allow you to open the car window while in place)

because a younger baby's immature bones and connective tissue mean she'll be less able to cope with the extra stresses of a forward-facing position in a frontal collision and will be at greater risk of serious injury.

As an absolute minimum, stick with a rear-facing seat until your baby is at least 12 months old and ideally has been sitting unaided for three months. Just because your baby reaches 9 kg and is therefore the minimum weight for the next stage, Group 1 seats, isn't a good enough reason to switch.

It is not a safety issue if your baby's knees are bent or his feet touch the back seat of the car. The only compelling reason to move a baby out of a Group 0+ seat before 12 months is if he has exceeded the maximum weight for his rear-facing seat or if his eye level is above the seat top. If this happens with your baby, consider one of the new 'rear-facing-for-longer seats', rather than moving him forward facing early. For more on Group 1 seats, see page 181.

As a response to the expected change in the law, we think there will soon be more 'rear-facing-for-longer' models on the market in the UK, in order to comply with new regulations.

IN-CAR ACCESSORIES

SUN BLINDS

Most babies get grouchy if the sun glares through side windows into their eyes and these are a cheap way of reducing some resulting tears. Roller-blind versions stay in place better than suction-pad ones; you can choose to pull them down or roll them up as needed and they're less likely to fall off and get trampled in the foot well. You can also buy a blind for the rear windscreen if you find you need it.

BABY VIEWING MIRROR

When driving, it can be hard to check on a baby in a rear-facing seat. A large mirror can be positioned above her so you can frequently glance to check how she is. Most mirrors fit on to the rear headrest with adjustable straps; if you don't have rear headrests, these won't be an option. You can get some

THE CAR SEAT GOLDEN RULES

Forgive us for repeating ourselves but this is so important that we want to reiterate the golden rules for car seats:

* *Check compatibility with your car.*
* *Install correctly; get help and advice.*
* *Rear seat centre*, where possible, is the safest position for a car seat and a rear-facing seat should never, ever go in the front if there's an airbag.
* *Babies should stay rear facing as long as possible.*
* *The harness should be checked every journey and adjusted as needed* It must be snug to your baby (remember also to adjust its height as your baby grows – it should be parallel to or just below her shoulders).

---

that attach by suction to the rear windscreen, but they tend to be small and hard to position. This is something you can buy later on; first see how you manage without.

'BABY ON BOARD' SIGNS

You either love them or hate them. We're still wondering what they're actually for. One theory is they alert emergency services to search for a baby in the event of a serious accident. We don't buy this; if the car is in such a bad way that the baby's seat and gubbins aren't visible, then we doubt that a small yellow sign stuck on with a suction pad is going to still be in place. And anyway, emergency services are trained to search the scene of an accident thoroughly – sign or no sign.

※ **Baby Viewing Mirror**
Easyview. Happy Mummy

Another idea is that they're there to ask other drivers to be patient with any erratic driving – fair enough but we doubt that most drivers care if you're dealing with a screaming infant who's just vomited over the back seat. Perhaps they're simply a badge of honour to tell the world you've got a baby? If so, and that floats your boat, don't let us stop you but they really aren't a necessity.

9

SAFETY ESSENTIALS AND MEDICAL EQUIPMENT

KEEPING YOUR BABY SAFE

Home safety for your family isn't just about stair gates and plug socket covers once your baby starts to get mobile; even before he arrives, there are a few things you can do to keep him safe.

Consider buying and fitting smoke alarms if you don't already have at least one on each level of your home; these should have a British Standards kitemark on them. Your local fire brigade should offer a free 'Home Fire Risk Assessment'

SHOPPING LIST

- ✓ Smoke and carbon monoxide detectors *(if not already in place)*
- ✓ Baby monitor*
- ✓ Childproofing items appropriate to your home
- ✓ First aid and medicine kit
- ✓ Thermometer
- ? Medicine dispensing syringe or dummy
- ? Nasal aspirator

(unless your home is very small)

service, where someone will come and check your home for any fire safety issues and can advise on the positioning of smoke alarms. Some families will be eligible for free alarms after this visit. Otherwise, alarns are inexpensive to buy and could give you crucial extra time if you need to get yourselves and your baby out of the house in the event of a fire.

Remember to replace the batteries every year and undertake regular checks (most models have a button you press to test the alarm is functioning).

A small, domestic fire extinguisher or two would also be a wise buy; locate one in the kitchen and, if your home is on two floors, keep one upstairs.

Think about escape routes, too, should a fire occur. For further advice on fire safety, see direct.gov.uk/firekills.

A carbon monoxide detector is another vital purchase; install it near the boiler and/or any gas fires and it will alert you should yours leak this dangerous gas, which has no colour, taste or smell and can prove fatal. See co-bealarmed.co.uk for more information.

BABY MONITORS

These devices allow you to keep a check on your baby when he is sleeping (or at least supposed to be) in a different room to you. You can get an idea as to whether he's drifted off (finally!)/woken-up (already!)/is crying (oh heck not feeding time again?).

Some monitors boast extra features, from live video streaming of your baby (think 'infant Big Brother') and talk-back functions, to light shows and alarms that go off if your baby stops breathing.

Do you really need one?

Our own parents managed without monitors but they've become a must-have for most modern mums and dads. If you live in anything other than the tiniest of homes and have the TV, radio or music on in the living room, you probably won't hear your baby crying in the bedroom, so a monitor will provide peace of mind.

When do you need it?

You won't use it until your baby starts sleeping in a different room to you so if, like most parents, you'll keep your baby close by for the first few weeks, you don't need to buy one straight away. If you do purchase a monitor before the birth, keep the packaging and receipt in case once your newborn arrives you feel more or less protective than you expected and want a different type of monitor.

THE MAIN BUYING DECISIONS:

Digital or analogue?

✳ **Digital Baby Monitor**
££ BT 200 (reliable digital monitor with talkback) •
£££ BT Digital Baby Monitor/Pacifier (extra features to soothe your baby)

Most monitors are now digital rather than analogue with the exception of a few cheaper models and some video monitors. Analogue monitors suffer more interference from other devices than their digital counterparts, so if you live in a block of flats and are buying an analogue monitor, choose one with quite a few channels to prevent cross-interference between nearby monitors and yours (it's awful to have to worry about your neighbours' monitors picking up that argument with your partner about who is more tired!).

Although concerns about the safety of digital devices in the home have been dismissed by the Health Protection Agency, for extra peace of mind, you could place the monitoring unit at least a metre from your baby.

Video or audio?

✳ **Video Monitor Summer Infant Baby Touch** (with pan, tilt and zoom and touch screen)

Critics say video monitors make it easy to become overly obsessed with checking on your little one and are expensive, but they can also be genuinely useful. They allow you to take a quick look at your baby without disturbing him, so you could see whether there's an obvious cause if he's crying or whether he's nodded off yet. The picture is transmitted to a portable handheld unit.

Video monitors are also effective for keeping an occasional eye on older children playing in another room.

Increasingly, video monitors have the same sorts of additional features as the more sophisticated audio ones – talkback, lullaby players and the like.

Movement/breathing or standard monitor?

Movement monitors have a sensor pad that sits under the cot mattress and detects movement when a baby breathes. Some monitors tick with every move, but all have an alarm that goes off if no movement is detected after a certain period, usually 20 seconds.

Some people think these monitors prey on parents' fears – the main criticism being that one wouldn't warn you in time to do something if your baby stopped breathing (a choking baby could still be moving) and most medics say they're unnecessary for healthy full-term babies. They're also prone to false alarms, causing unnecessary panic (following the instructions carefully, particularly about where to position the sensor pad, helps limit these). Despite this, some parents find movement monitors highly reassuring, especially those whose babies had breathing difficulties at birth.

Movement Monitor
Angelcare (movement and audio monitor combined), **Tomy TD monitors** (have an optional movement sensor pad, sold separately, which you can add on to their digital audio or video monitors if you feel the need once your baby arrives)

Look for:
Essential:
✳ *Clarity* You need to be able to hear your baby well without annoying interference. Note that more expensive models tend to provide a clearer signal with less interference.
✳ *For video monitors* Make sure your choice has an infra-red camera for when it's dark in the nursery and a large enough screen on the handheld parent unit so you can see what your baby is doing. Look, too, for a function that allows you to turn the screen off, either to conserve power or prevent the glow annoying you at night, or in case you want to use the monitor on an audio-only basis.

Useful:
✳ *Dual power* This allows you the option of either plugging the monitor's parent unit into the mains, or to move between rooms using it in battery-power mode. In reality, most parents use their unit in battery-power mode in the daytime or evening and then plug it into the mains overnight in their own bedroom. Most modern monitors come with rechargeable batteries; avoid any that do not. A battery power option is also useful for the 'baby unit' if, like one of

us, you have a house strangely prone to power cuts. Check there's a low power warning light for when the batteries run out. If portability is important to you, prioritise a model that's easy to carry or has a belt clip.

❋ *A choice of channels* This will help limit interference if you're buying an analogue monitor. Two or three should suffice (digital models often have many more).

❋ *A range appropriate for your home and needs* Manufacturers sometimes quote both an indoor and outdoor range; 30 m indoors and 100 m outdoors will usually suffice but if you have a very large garden or a mansion-sized home, look for more. A lot of monitors nowadays come with a 300 m outdoor range as standard.

❋ *A talkback function* Sometimes babies will settle back to sleep after hearing a familiar voice and a talkback function allows you to provide reassurance without necessarily going into the room. It certainly doesn't obviate the need for night feeds or the like, but it can be useful, for example, to persuade an early-waking toddler that the day doesn't start at 5 a.m., without having to leave the warmth of your bed. If we had to choose one non-essential but particularly worthwhile feature for a monitor, it'd be this.

❋ *Automatic lullaby function* This means you can prompt your monitor to play soothing music when your baby makes a noise – either remotely from your parent unit on some models, but only by going into the nursery and pressing a button on the baby unit on others. This might or might not calm him but consider that the music could well annoy you. Potentially worthwhile for some little ones but don't worry too much if the model you want doesn't have this.

❋ *Light display/vibrate alert* These allow you to be alerted to your baby's cries by flashing lights on your receiving unit or vibrations, instead of sound. This probably isn't something you'll use regularly, but could be helpful during a dinner party or if you make important work calls at home and don't want sudden crying to be audible. With a light display, you obviously need to remember to keep an eye on the monitor otherwise it rather defeats the purpose.

* *With video monitors, a pan, tilt and zoom function* will allow you to observe your baby better if he moves around in his cot. You may also have the option to add additional cameras. This can be useful if you have another baby relatively soon after your first and they're in separate rooms and you'd like to be able to monitor both, or if you have older kids and want to keep an eye on activity in more than one room. If the foregoing are considerations, check that the monitor will, when relevant, automatically switch to the camera in the room where noise is coming from, as having to manually flick between cameras will be frustrating.

Don't pay extra for:

* *Integral nursery thermometers* Some monitors have a light on the parent unit that tells you when the nursery gets too cold or hot. Unless your baby's room is a vastly different temperature to the rest of the house, you'll have an idea of whether it's too hot or too cold without this feature.
* *Integral nightlights* You can buy separate ones cheaply and those on monitors tend to be pretty feeble anyway.
* *Out-of-range warning* Unnecessary; just test the range by getting someone to holler down the unit beside your baby once and check roughly where in your garden you can hear him or her on the parent unit. You're unlikely to want to leave your baby alone at the sort of distances most monitors will no longer work at anyway.

CHILDPROOFING

The extent to which you need to childproof your house will depend on the nature of your home and its contents, your attitude to parenting, your baby's age and even, to an extent, his personality.

If your house is brimming with precious knick-knacks or particularly full of dangers – steep steps to tumble down, sharp-cornered furniture, open fireplaces and the like – you'll need to be particularly rigorous. Likewise, once your baby starts being mobile, if he turns out to have an adventurous,

inquisitive nature, you'll probably need to go a step further than if he's the cautious kind.

It's hard to know where to draw the line though. Go too far and your child won't learn what he can and can't touch and will cause category five hurricane-style chaos when visiting places that aren't childproofed. Don't go far enough and obviously you risk preventable injuries (or worse) and might well spend the first few years of your child's life constantly telling him not to touch things (quite tiresome for both you and him).

OUR RECOMMENDED APPROACH
Step 1.
Identify clear danger spots in your house (fireplaces, staircases and steep steps, large expanses of glass and low windows) and childproof them as soon as your baby shows signs of moving around. This includes removing or making safe anything that could cause serious injury.

We also recommend fitting cabinet locks to a couple of kitchen cupboards so that you have a safe, inaccessible place to store cleaning products and that bone china dinner service you probably never use but don't want your baby to employ as a missile. Medicines and any other potentially harmful substances should also be kept out of reach in a childproof cupboard or container.

Other essential needs like stair gates and window and fire guards will depend on your individual home.

Step 2.
Once your baby gets more mobile, move precious items or those you don't want tipping on the floor/ripping up, out of his reach. Get down on your hands and knees for an idea of what your baby can get to – you might notice a few things you'd missed from your adult viewpoint.

Review things as your baby starts to touch loftier shelves and drawers. You might be able to avoid childproofing one or two rooms, such as a home office, by simply keeping the door shut (and locked once he's older), when your baby is around.

Step 3.
Wait and see what, if anything else, becomes problematic. Baby product companies might make you feel you need to cover the entire house in cottonwool but you don't. Some of the minor accidents items such as table corner cushions prevent can be upsetting but most children learn pretty quickly to be careful.

The good news is that most childproofing products are relatively cheap, the bad news is that many are rather ugly. Obviously if an item is truly necessary to keep your child safe, aesthetics are going to have to take second place for a while.

When do you need to do it?
Only when your baby shows signs of getting mobile, this varies but can be as early as five or six months of age.

CHILDPROOFING ESSENTIALS

STAIR GATES
Unless you live in a one-level flat or bungalow, these prevent a baby accessing the staircase; they also can be used across doorways to keep little ones inside or out of a room.

Most parents choose to place gates at both the top and bottom of the stairs. Check what size openings a particular gate is suitable for and whether it will fit your stairs or doorways before buying.

Types:
* **Fixed** These permanently attach to the wall. They take longer to fit as they must be screwed in, so you'll have to get your drill out, but they're a sturdy, secure choice.
* **Pressure-fit** Easier to fit as they don't require wall-mountings or fixings, but you'll need flat walls or banisters to attach the gate to. Some have a gauge to show that the pressure is sufficiently strong but if the gate is fitted according to instructions, this feature isn't necessary.
* **'Rollerblind'** Reinforced mesh pulls across from one side of the staircase to the other where it attaches to a fixing,

Stair gates are well-suited to secondhand purchase, but check fitting instructions and all screws and fixings are included.

✳ **Stair Gate**
Lascal Kiddyguard (fits openings from 10–130 cm)

✳ *For unusual, narrow or wider stairs and doorways:* **Babydan ConfigureGate** • *Standard gates:* **Babydan, Bettacare, Lindam.**

forming a barrier. These are currently only made by Lascal. They're especially good for awkward and wider staircases and offer the greatest flexibility. They fold away when not needed and don't have trip bars to fall over (a bar that sits across the bottom of the gate and doesn't open – it's easy to trip over them).

Whichever style you choose, look for a one-handed release, as you'll often be carrying your baby (or something else) when you use it. Some models have auto-close doors, which swing shut even if you forget to close them.

Measure up before considering your options and don't forget you may need an extension kit if the gate you want isn't quite wide enough.

DRAWER/CUPBOARD LOCKS

Locking a few of your cupboards means you can keep cleaning products, your best china and knives out of reach. You needn't lock all of them. Locks can be self-adhesive or screw in; some are visible on the outside of the cupboard or drawer and some fit on the inside.

✳ **Basic Door/Drawer Catches**
Clippasafe or Safety 1st (*the basic versions allow doors/drawers to open slightly, so don't prevent minor finger trappings, but your child will learn quickly to stay away. Both these companies sell anti-finger-trap versions.*), **Babydan magnetic locks**

Basic door catches are cheap and effective but need screwing in – a pain if you have a lot to fit. Multi-purpose self-adhesive locks just stick on but they sit on the outside of the cupboard so can look ugly; some are less obtrusive than others. For double cupboards with protruding handles, slide locks are very effective. We prefer the ones that have a squeezy button in the middle and separate out rather than the sliding ones, which are more clumsy looking.

Sooner or later most children work out how to crack locks but by this stage hopefully they will have developed some sense of danger. Magnetic locks are the most secure; these are particularly suited to medicine cabinets as you can only open them with the key provided. They're also invisible from the outside of the cupboard and often self-adhesive so easy to fit.

OTHER CHILDPROOFING ITEMS

Whether you need these items depends on your home: a few might be vital, others useful, some unnecessary.

FIREGUARDS
This is essential if you have a fireplace you'll use when your baby is around. Look for a guard that attaches securely to the wall so a toddler can't pull it over, and with a top so that your little darling can't lob things into the fire.

HOB GUARDS
These clear shield-like heatproof screens are designed to prevent children reaching up to touch a hot hob or grabbing pan handles (whose contents could spill onto them). In any case, it makes sense to keep babies away from the cooker, either out of the room or in a playpen, and to keep pan handles away from the edge by using only the back burners.

OVEN DOOR GUARD
If you have a low oven and the glass gets hot when it's on, you can get a heat-resistant guard to stick on the oven door.

WINDOW LOCKS
These let windows be opened a little to allow air in but not far enough that a child could fall out. Whether you need them depends on the style of your windows. Some locks cannot be fitted to metal-framed or PVC double glazed windows so check before buying.

FRIDGE/FREEZER LOCK
Small children love to open fridges and whilst this isn't dangerous, it can be inconvenient to have the contents emptied onto the floor, or worse still, the freezer door left open. The multi-purpose stick-on locks mentioned previously will do the same job as specific fridge locks. Again, see if your child starts playing around with the fridge or freezer before buying one – he might not.

✳ **Fireguard**
Bettacare, BabyDan

✳ **Hob Guard**
Prince Lionheart

COOKER LOCKS

Stick-on locks can stop a baby or toddler opening a low oven's door. Ensure your oven is heat proof. You can also buy covers for cooker knobs so that your little one can't accidentally turn the hob or oven on. Until you've checked the guards will fit your cooker, don't throw away the packaging. Again, if you keep your baby supervised when the oven is on, or it is too high for him to reach and he wouldn't be able to climb up on something, you won't need them.

If you'll be bathing two children in the bath at once, you might need to get a tap cover to prevent small heads knocking against them. This is less of an issue if you have one child because you can sit him away from the taps.

TOILET LOCK

This stops your baby from opening the loo lid and putting his hands (or other items) into the toilet bowl or trapping fingers. Wait and see if this becomes a problem with your child. If your child goes through this phase, it probably won't last long regardless of whether or not you invest in a lock.

DOOR SLAM STOPPERS

These guards stop small hands getting slammed in doors. There are two types: the standard white u-shaped slam stoppers that need removing when you want to close the door and on/off stoppers that you fix to the doorpost.

CORNER CUSHIONS

Stick-on pads for furniture are only really necessary if your baby is particularly clumsy and/or you have furniture with very sharp corners at toddler head level. If you need them, transparent plastic versions don't look quite as awful as white plastic ones.

DVD, SATELLITE OR DIGITAL TV BOX COVERS

Babies and toddlers love to fiddle with these machines. A cover stops items being 'posted' into the dvd slot and prevents the machines operating. Even if you have a machine(s) with an integral child lock function, you'll still have to remember to turn it on.

GLASS SAFETY FILM

This is essential if you have expanses of glass in doors, furniture or accessible windows that aren't modern safety

glass. The film sticks onto the glass so that if it breaks, it won't split into shards.

CAT NET
An essential for cat owners unless you can guarantee that the door to the room in which your baby sleeps will always be shut, so the cat can't get in.

BLIND CORD WINDERS
Designed to prevent risk of strangulation from blind cords, these hold the excess cord neatly within a small box. You can manage without by just tying the cords out of reach but the winders are cheap, safer and look tidier.

PLAYPEN
This is a sensible way to keep your baby safe if you need to answer the door, go to the loo and so forth. However, a playpen can be expensive and take up a lot of space, and the time when it is useful may be very limited; it isn't necessary before your baby is mobile (and even in the early stages of mobility you can strap him into a bouncy chair for a short while), and once he's walking he'll probably hate being 'imprisoned' in a pen.

Pens can be a godsend if you have two children very close in age, as you can keep the older toddler from accidentally trampling on or pulling the hair of the baby without you having to watch them every second of the day. One can also help you keep an older child's toys that may be choking hazards for a baby, away from the younger one.

Generally, instead of a playpen, we recommend using a travel cot. It works just as well and is multi-functional so offers significantly better value for money.

If you have the space, an alternative is to fit a room divider, creating a larger, childproofed area in which your baby can play safely.

Playpen
BabyDan (can be configured as a traditional playpen or a room divider and you can add extra panels)

Steer clear of:
✳ *Plug socket covers* These blank plug socket covers are designed to prevent babies sticking items into plugholes,

Brief relatives, carers and houseguests about child-safety issues. Those who don't have small children or haven't had them recently might need reminding of some of the precautions you like to take such as keeping the stair gate closed.

potentially electrocuting themselves. According to the Royal Society for the Prevention of Accidents (ROSPA), the modern UK 13-amp power sockets (made to BS 1363:1995), which most people have in their homes, incorporate a shutter mechanism that prevenst inappropriate access to the live connectors so socket covers are unnecessary. If you're in doubt about whether your sockets conform to these standards and want to fit covers, avoid any with designs printed on them, which might attract your child's attention.

✷ *Radiator guards* With most central heating systems, you can turn the temperature down slightly so that the radiators remain effective but not so hot that burns could occur (this also helps the environment, too).

✷ *Cable tidies* These keep loose wiring from electrical appliances and lamps tucked away. You're unlikely to need them as you can almost always just hide the cables out of reach behind the appliance or furniture.

HEALTH ITEMS

Sadly, minor illnesses and injuries go with the territory with babies and toddlers. That scouting motto 'be prepared' is a wise one here: if you keep essential medicines and first-aid supplies in stock and to hand, you could save yourself a stressful dash to the all-night chemist or a frantic search for bandages.

FIRST-AID AND MEDICINE KITS

You can buy a first-aid kit suitable for children (and add essential medicines) or assemble your own using our list. Tell babysitters and other carers where it is. You might want to stick useful telephone numbers to the lid such as that of your GP, NHS Direct (0845 4647), the Emergency Services (999) and your mobile number.

Some parents also like to keep a stock of homeopathic remedies. Examples are chamomilla for teething, calendula tablets and cream for nappy rash and as an antiseptic, and arnica for bumps and bruises.

WHAT TO PUT IN YOUR FIRST-AID KIT

✓ Infant pain reliever – Calpol, Nurofen for Children or similar (neither can be used for very new babies so check the instructions)
✓ Antiseptic cream or spray
✓ Tweezers and scissors
✓ Calamine or aloe vera for sunburn and rashes
✓ Insect bite reliever/antihistamine cream suitable for children
✓ Bandages, dressings and plasters plus medical adhesive tape
✓ Thermometer – see below
✓ Burn relief spray

It's sensible to take a short paediatric first-aid course before your baby arrives. This will cover crucial skills such as infant resuscitation and how to deal with choking incidents. There are a number of providers who run courses; try redcrossfirstaidtraining. co.uk

THERMOMETERS

There are three types of thermometer available for taking young children's temperatures.

Types:

❖ *Standard* These are relatively cheap and can be used orally, under the armpit or, if you aren't squeamish, rectally. They take around 30 seconds to get a reading although it can be challenging to keep one in place with a struggling baby for that long. Avoid mercury thermometers – digital ones are easier to use.

❖ *Digital in-ear /forehead* Pricier but more accurate, these give a very quick reading (most after a second or two) and can be used on babies, children and adults. Crucially, they can be used easily on a sleeping child without disturbing him.

❖ *Forehead strips* that you hold in place until a reading comes up. They're very cheap but not terribly accurate and hard to use if a baby is wriggling around, so we don't recommend them.

Thermometer Brother Max 3-in-1 Digital

Verdict: A digital in-ear or forehead thermometer is worth investing in as you will get years of use out of it.

※ Nasal Aspirator
Nuk, Summer Infant

MEDICINE DISPENSERS

There are two versions of these: ones that resemble mini syringes and ones that are a cross between a dummy and a mini-baby bottle. With the syringes you squirt the medicine directly into your baby's mouth and hope he doesn't spit it out. With the dummy-style ones, you put the medicine into a little container at the back of the teat and your baby sucks it out. Some babies who aren't used to bottles or dummies will not accept the latter type. Both versions are cheap (under £5) so it might be worth getting one of each in case one works better than the other with your baby.

NASAL ASPIRATORS

Babies can't blow their noses so can become particularly bunged up when they have a cold. Extracting snot from a baby's nose isn't the most delightful of tasks, but these do suck nasal mucous out effectively. Choose one with a wide bulb so that you can't force it up too far and cause damage. Useful but not essential.

HOME BABY SCALES

We can't think of a single reason why you'd need your own. Don't buy them! Normal healthy babies are weighed frequently enough by the health visitor; weigh any more often at home and you'll risk getting hung up on the issue. Babies whose weight gain is worryingly poor should be monitored by a health professional. And what's so difficult about weighing your baby on normal scales? Step on once holding him, once without, and subtract the difference.

TOYS AND PLAYING

TOYS

Newborns spend much of their time sleeping and feeding but as the weeks pass, the stretches when they're awake and need entertaining lengthen. Raiding the toyshop is enormous fun but don't go overboard. Younger babies are perfectly content with a few carefully chosen items and you will probably be given plenty of toys as gifts anyway. And even when your baby is older, he'll enjoy playing with your mobile phone/car keys/ pots and pans as much as with expensive toys. Here are some guiding principles for choosing toys:

✳ Expensive doesn't necessarily mean more appealing to your baby; the box the toy comes in is often of more interest.

SHOPPING LIST

✓ A small selection of toys
? Sleep aid
? Bouncy chair
? Baby swing
? Playnest
✗ Sit-in activity centre
✗ Walker

Newborn Toys
Manhattan Toy/ Wimmer
Ferguson Mind Shapes
range, Tiny Love's Black
and White Bumper Book

Mobiles
Tiny Love Symphony in
Motion (offers both
movement and music and
the music box is useful
even once the mobile
must be removed for
safety reasons).
Manhattan Toy/ Wimmer
Ferguson Infant Stim
Mobile (award-winning
black and white themed
mobile which appeals to
newborns, non-musical)

❋ Always choose age-appropriate toys for your baby; be guided not only by the age range given on the packaging, but also by your baby's own development.

❋ Toys should be easy to clean – either wipeable or washable – and for young babies, be chunky with large pieces. Avoid toys with small parts (like detachable 'eyes'), sharp edges and strings longer than 30 cm [12 in]. Keep toys clean and in good condition.

❋ Buy one or two items that attach to the pram or car seat; they won't fall into a puddle or car foot well, which invariably leads to crying.

❋ Accept that having at least some garish toys strewn across your house is an inevitable part of parenthood; they'll appeal to your baby even if they don't appeal to your sense of style.

❋ Hold back from buying a few bigger items in case generous relatives want guidance on gifts to buy for junior.

❋ If your child becomes particularly attached to a specific small toy or teddy, buy a spare to prevent meltdowns if it gets lost.

RECOMMENDED TOYS FOR BABIES

Here are some of our favourite things to entertain babies during their first year:

From birth

❋ *Toys with bold black and white imagery* Newborns respond better to these than to busily patterned toys.

❋ *A musical mobile* Mobiles transfix many infants but bear in mind that a mobile needs to be removed from the cot once your baby starts sitting up – as early as five months. Choose one where the interesting bits face downward as your baby will be lying underneath it; some mobiles are pointlessly dull from underneath!

❋ *A baby gym* This bizarre name conjures up some sort of infant health club but these are simply padded mats with integral toys dangling from an arch above, sometimes with a musical function. Most babies happily lounge about on

them, gazing at the dangling toys and later on try to bat and catch them. They're quite expensive but very worthwhile.

From three months
* *'Shaky' toys and rattles.*
* *Jangly, linked rings.*
* *Brightly-coloured fabric books.*
* *Teething rings.*
* *Multi-purpose soft activity toys* The best are small but packed with features to hold a baby's interest – crinkly fabrics and textures, bells, squeaky bits, baby-safe mirrors, that kind of thing. They're very portable and some attach to a car seat or pram.

From six months
* *Toy mobile phones and keys* (but they'll still try and grab yours!).
* *Toys with buttons* to press to elicit sounds and lights.
* *Bath toys.*
* *Baby mirror.*
* *Books with vinyl or board pages.*

From nine months
* *Stacking cups.*
* *Push and/or pull-alongs.*
* *Large building blocks.*
* *Beakers, cups and floating toys.*

Baby Gym
Tiny Love Gymini range, Baby Einstein Seek and Discover Gym

Activity Toys
Whoozit Activity Spiral, Baby Whoozit, Bondie Bird Playwrap

SLEEP AIDS

As we said in an earlier chapter, sleep is a key issue for new parents with a baby on the scene and you'll want to do everything you can to maximise the amount you get.

Nothing can magically make your baby not wake for feeds or due to discomfort from a leaky nappy but some products do seem to be able to soothe little ones to sleep quite effectively. There are a couple of sleep aids, which we think are worth considering – you'd only need one of these.

Sleep Aid

Ewan The Dream Sheep, Prince Lionheart Slumberbear

You might also find that once you have used a particular sleep aid for a while the sound it makes acts as a trigger for your baby to doze off. This can be very effective but does mean that if you don't remember to take the product with you whenever and wherever your baby needs to sleep, you might find that without it, she can't.

PRODUCT SHOWCASE

Ewan The Dream Sheep is a clever little product, which takes the teddy bear to new levels of assisting your baby to sleep. Ewan is not only a cuddly looking sheep, he emits gentle womb-like noises and a soft red glow, to calm and reassure your baby. It all sounds a bit left-field but feedback from parents is very positive; Ewan has genuinely helped their baby sleep better. **Prince Lionheart's Slumberbear** is a similar product without the red glow but with a wider variety of soothing sounds, which can be set to trigger automatically when your baby stirs. Both are safe for newborns (not all teddy bears are) and, at around £25, either would make a lovely new baby gift.

CHAIRS AND ROCKERS

Having a few different places to put your baby when she isn't being cuddled or fed will help to keep her content. A bouncy chair or rocker is a staple of most new parents' homes – a place for short naps, for feeding during early weaning and a vantage point, letting babies get a better view of the world. Chairs either bounce or rock with your baby's movement and some have extras like toy bars and vibrating or music functions. They're almost all suitable from birth until six to nine months, depending on the model and your baby's weight.

As with car seats, you shouldn't leave a newborn in a baby chair for more than a couple of hours unless the chair reclines flat or almost flat. Certainly, they are not great places for napping compared to a flat carrycot, Moses basket or cot.

Baby bean bags, sold as an alternative to bouncy chairs, must be designed specifically for newborns, have a harness and be firm and supportive.

Do you really need one?

A baby chair is definitely useful although not essential.

When do you need it?

Worth buying before the birth, although it should only be used for your newborn for short periods if it can't be made flat or almost flat.

Types

* ❊ *Bouncy chairs* These have a fabric seat stretched over a wire frame. The baby's movement makes the chair bounce.
* ❊ *Rockers* More sophisticated and usually more expensive chairs, these are well-padded with several seat positions, usually including somewhat of a recline. You make these move by gently rocking them.

Look for:
Essential:
* ❊ *A secure harness.*
* ❊ *A washable or wipeable seat*, especially if you might use it for feeding later on.

✳ **Bouncy Chairs, Rockers or Baby Chairs**
££ Chicco Mia Range (comfortable, lie-flat) •
£££ Babybjorn Babysitter (suitable from birth up to age two)

✳ **£ Mothercare Spring Bouncer** (basic but does the job) • **£££ Beaba Up and Down Bouncer** (height adjustable so your baby can be at sofa level)

Larger baby toys such as activity centres and swings can keep babies entertained when you need to get on with chores but are expensive and most will only be of interest for a few months. With this is mind, borrow or buy second-hand. Such items also take up a lot of space, so hold off and see what you'll find useful and have room for.

Useful:

❈ *A reclining seat* A chair that can be upright or lie-flat/almost flat is preferable for longer periods of use and can double up as a place for naps.

❈ *A rocking base that can also be fixed* Some babies are soothed by rocking, others aren't, so having a choice is best.

❈ *A vibrating function* Some chairs have a vibrate function designed to settle babies. Not all babies like this though.

❈ *A chair* that folds flat for travel or storage.

❈ *A toy bar* Ensure this detaches as it could get in your way when taking your baby in and out.

❈ *Carry handles* These make it easier to move the chair around.

Don't worry about:

❈ *Too many extras* This chair is only going to last from birth to six months so don't spend a fortune on something very flashy.

SIT-IN ACTIVITY CENTRES

With these, your baby sits in a fabric seat surrounded by a ring featuring assorted toys and activities. They're much safer than wheeled versions known as walkers (see opposite page). Overall, however, we still don't recommend splashing out on one as they're bulky, unattractive, expensive and only useful for a short period of time. By all means borrow one, though as an extra place for your baby to play for short periods, if you have space.

 Playnest
Galt

PLAYNESTS

These consist of a large inflatable or cushioned ring, with toys attached. They provide extra support during the stage when your baby can't sit unaided without toppling over rather spectacularly but would like to watch the world. Later on, they make a fun place to climb in and out of (perhaps from around five to ten months).

BABY SWINGS

Some parents absolutely swear by these motorised indoor swings to settle fussing or crying newborns. We aren't huge

fans for the same reasons as for activity centres. Only consider one if you have a very unsettled baby and nothing else works. Again, given the cost and lack of longevity, it might be better to buy second-hand or borrow.

SIT-IN WALKERS

There are concerns about sit-in baby walkers as they give babies a level of mobility they aren't naturally ready for and can be dangerous. The Association of Paediatric Chartered Physiotherapists warns against them as they encourage babies to walk in an unnatural tiptoe position and their use reduces the time babies spend on the floor practising body control in the natural developmental way. There is no evidence that these actually help a baby to walk earlier, anyway. Steer clear. A cheaper, simple push-along trolley (the sort with a tray of bricks) can be fun, though.

DOOR BOUNCERS

These allow your baby to bounce around in a doorway, usually triggering giggles from said little one (although a few babies dislike them). They look fun, yes, but again The Association of Paediatric Chartered Physiotherapists isn't keen, as they encourage babies to bounce on their tiptoes and arch their back unnaturally.

Create a 'treasure basket'. Once your baby is able to get about a little, a fantastic, cheap way to keep her happily occupied, is to fill a large container with items of varied shapes and textures (obviously everything must be baby safe – no loose or broken parts which could be choking hazards). Include wooden and metal spoons, flannels, a nail brush, an egg whisk, a sponge – the possibilities are endless. Always keep a close eye on your baby/ toddler when she is playing with the basket's contents.

CHAPTER 11

TRAVEL EQUIPMENT AND ACCESSORIES

FOR PARENTS ON THE GO

Travelling light is rarely possible for new parents; no matter whether you holiday locally or abroad, you're going to be dragging piles of baby paraphernalia along for the ride for the foreseeable future.

TRAVEL COTS

Travel cots have been particular culprits when it comes to using up luggage allowance. Conventional models are bulky and weighty (typically around 10 kg), and certainly not something you'd want to drag around whilst trekking through the Himalayas (admittedly not something most new parents contemplate).

SHOPPING LIST

- ? Travel cot
- ? Portable highchair/booster seat
- ✓ Sun cream and insect protection
- ? UV protection clothes
- ? Swimming nappies
- ? Swimming aids
- ✗ Sun protection tents/shelters

Thankfully, innovative and much more portable designs have hit the market recently, although for reasons we'll go into below, for some parents, the conventional type will still be preferable.

Do you really need one?

For the first few months, you can use your carrycot or Moses basket (provided you have one); if you don't, then yes, you might need a travel cot. After that it depends on your travel plans. Most hotels, self-catering properties and B&Bs can provide cots, obviating the need to drag your own along. If you'll stay somewhere where this won't be the case, perhaps with friends or relatives, then you probably will need one. Or you could look at whether there's a baby equipment rental service local to your destination. To extract more 'value' from a travel cot, it can be used as a place for downstairs naps in the early months, or as a playpen (see page 155). A money-saving option is to club together with friends and share one, provided you all won't be away at the same time.

When do you need it?

Wait and buy one if and when you need it.

TYPES OF TRAVEL COT

❊ *Conventional* These tend to be bulky and heavy (around 10 kg), although there are exceptions. However, they also are sturdy and easy to assemble. Conventional travel cots can also double as playpens, as they're relatively robust and most have see-through mesh sides. Their weight and size won't be a major issue if you mainly travel by car or the cot will be left assembled at your destination. Some come with a bassinette for newborns, a changing tray or integral toys.

❊ *Tent-style* Consisting of a fabric surround formed into a bed shape by poles threaded through the fabric, most can act as sun protection shelters outdoors. They're also light and compact (some as little as 2 kg) but can be tricky to assemble.

❊ *Pop-up* Very light (around 2 kg), compact and easy-to-use, these cots pop out of a carry bag and some have self-inflating 'air' mattresses. They're very easy to put up but take

✳ **Travel Cot**

Pop-up:

££ NS Associates
Travel Centre
(sometimes sold under
NScessity branding) ·

Conventional:

£££ Babybjorn

✳ *Pop-up*

££ Bushbaby Egg ·

Conventional:

£ Red Kite Sleep Tight
Travel Cot · ££ Graco
Contour · £££ Nuna
Sena (the full-size one,
not the mini version
which won't last long
enough)

a little practice to pack away and because they aren't so sturdy (more boisterous toddlers could topple theirs), they might need to be placed between a sofa and bed or similar. For this reason they aren't ideal for use as playpens.

How to decide:

Think about the places you'll travel to and your usual mode of transport. If you'll mainly use trains, planes or coaches, then minimising weight and bulk will be wise.

Look for:
Essential:

✳ *Ease-of-use* You can buy the best-looking, fully-featured travel cot but if it requires a degree in engineering to erect or collapse, you'll be cursing it when you arrive at your destination late at night, desperate to get you and your baby to bed quickly. Check product reviews online for others views and get a demo in-store.

✳ *A decent size when assembled* If it isn't big enough for a two- or three year old, it won't last until your baby can sleep in a proper bed, meaning you'd need to buy a second, larger travel cot later on. Consult the marketing literature for the cot's age range recommendation. Koo-di's pop-up models are guilty of this (the newborn version lasts until six months and even the larger one only until 18 months) and are therefore best avoided. Also be wary of square mattresses as your normal cot sheets might not fit.

Useful:

✳ *Compact size when folded up* Check to see how much luggage/boot/cupboard space the cot takes up when it's packed away.

✳ *Light weight* (essential if you travel by plane or train a lot). Conventional models tend to be heavy, weighing as much as 13 kg, pop-ups and tent-style cots as little as 2 kg. There are exceptions; Babybjorn does a conventional-style model that comes in at around 4 kg and packs down relatively small, although not as small as tent and pop-up versions.

✳ *Multi-use potential* Some parents use a travel cot as a

playpen when their baby gets mobile; more robust conventional models are better suited for this than pop-ups and tents. Look for mesh sides for better visibility. Most pop-ups and tents double as UV sun protection shelters, which we don't think are necessary anyway (see below).

* *A wheeled carrybag* This will improve portability with heavier conventional models.
* *A self-inflating mattress* will be more convenient and less bulky for you and more comfortable for your baby but isn't often available.
* *Mosquito netting* This isn't usually an option on conventional cots so you'll have to add a separate insect net where biters are a concern. Most pop-up and tent travel cots have this as standard.
* *A basinette* Some travel cots have a raised area for a younger baby so you can get yours in and out more easily, without bending over the cot side so much. These add weight and bulk and are only worthwhile if you'll use the cot a lot in the early months as they are not suitable for older babies.

Don't worry about:
* *A travel changing unit that fits on top of the travel cot* Just use the floor or your bed when you're away.
* *Fancy features* such as integral nightlights/music boxes/vibrating mattresses/toys. None of these are necessary and add extra weight and cost.
* *A spare or thicker mattress* Travel cots tend to come with either very thin vinyl-covered mattresses or, less commonly, inflatable ones. Some lack the comfort of standard cot mattresses but are adequate for occasional use. You can buy thicker travel mattresses but these are only worthwhile if the cot will be used very frequently in one place as they're bulky. Make sure the mattress fits the travel cot base well; the gap around the edge should be 4 cm or less.

Verdict: If you need a travel cot for 'serious' travel, go for a lightweight option; otherwise, consider a conventional one, which can double as a playpen.

PORTABLE HIGHCHAIRS AND BOOSTER SEATS

Once your baby reaches the weaning stage, you'll enter the literally murky world of the restaurant highchair. Whilst many are perfectly acceptable, some are so coated in the remnants of other babies' dinners, you'll think twice before putting your little darling in them. Taking your own portable highchair overcomes this. Even if you'd rather not take one along to restaurants, they're worthwhile for visiting friends' or relatives' houses and when you have other people's children round and need a second highchair.

Do you really need one?

They're actually less useful for holidays than might be expected as most hotels/restaurants/villas provide highchairs and they're an extra bit of luggage. However, ours got their money's worth of use at grandparents' houses and when other children were visiting. You could manage without but we think they're a worthwhile buy.

When do you need it?

Definitely not before the weaning stage (five to six months). Even in early weaning you can usually just spoon feed your baby on your knee or in their pushchair.

Types:

✳ *Plastic 'portable' highchair with tray* These are plastic seats with a harness that strap onto a standard chair. If you remove the tray, they double as a toddler booster seat. They last the whole period when your child needs some sort of highchair and are great value (£15 to £25). They tend to be quite garish and we've put those little inverted commas around 'portable' as they're bulky and therefore unsuitable for anything other than car travel. Some also have quite a few nooks and crannies in which food gathers.

✳ *Fabric dining chair harness* These loop around or over the chair back with a fabric harness to hold your baby in place. They pack away very small but can get dirty, so must be machine washable. They only really work for early weaning as once your baby wants/needs to self feed, they don't add

✴ **Plastic Portable Highchairs**
££ Beaba Alto (looks stylish and has no nooks and crannies!)

✴ £ First Years, Safety 1st • ££ Ikea's Antilop (see also page 73)

any height, so don't help your baby reach the table. They are, however, very cheap (around £10) so you could move onto a booster once you reach that stage.

- *'Clamp on' seat/ 'table seat'* These consist of a fabric seat suspended from a metal ring that clamps to the table. They are relatively light and compact but must be fitted carefully to ensure safety and can be difficult to keep clean.
- *Booster pad* (either light density foam or inflatable). Really glorified wipe-clean cushions but very effective at allowing toddlers better access to the table. Not suitable for younger babies given the lack of harness but some do at least have a basic safety lap belt. Some of this type of seat are inflatable, so they pack down smaller for portability.
- *Rigid booster seat* (usually wooden). These strap onto a dining chair, fitting most but not all chairs, and have an integral harness. They don't have a tray so your child eats at the table. Although manufacturers of the most commonly sold versions claim suitability from seven months, some parents find they aren't supportive enough for another month or two. They are, however, easy to clean and pack flat for holidays or restaurant trips.

Fabric Harness
£ Clippasafe Harness Highchair (more adaptable than others)

Clamp-on Seat
££ Phil&Teds Me Too and Lobster

Booster Pad
£ Prince Lionheart soft booster, First Years Inflatable booster

Rigid Booster
££/£££ Handysitt, Litaf

Look for:

As you can see none of the available options are perfect for all age groups and situations. To decide which might suit you best, think about how you travel (and therefore how important weight and bulk are), the age of your baby when you're buying and where you'll use the seat.

- *Adjustability* Check whether the seat and tray can be positioned at different heights. Will it adjust to fit all, or at least nearly all, shapes of dining chair?
- *Comfort and support* These are crucial especially for a younger baby who might only just be sitting up.
- *Ease of cleaning* As with standard highchairs, watch out for nooks and crannies and ensure materials are either machine-washable or wipeable.

Don't worry about:
- *Reclining seats.*

SUN AND INSECT PROTECTION

✳ Sun Cream
✿ Organic Children,
Green People, Lavera's
lotions, Dr Haushka •
Sunsense (not organic but
low on chemicals, high on
protection and good for
children with eczema or
sensitive skin)

Sun creams and insect repellents can contain harsh chemicals so we recommend going organic, where possible. Our philosophy is that if you can skip the chemicals without compromising on effectiveness, and often without spending much extra, why wouldn't you?

SUN CREAMS
You probably won't need sun cream for your baby initially, as she shouldn't be in direct sunlight during her first few months. Choose a gentle formulation suitable for sensitive baby skin. There are several ranges of organic suncream for children, some of which are available in supermarkets and high street stores.

INSECT REPELLENTS
These can contain very strong chemicals and are often labelled as unsuitable for young children. There's particular concern about the use of the chemical DEET. Hunt around and you can find natural insect repellents that can be used on young children. Mosi-Guard is one such natural formulation and fairly widely available. Even when using insect repellent, it's wise to keep your baby's skin covered when most at risk.

If your baby does get bitten, a soothing witch hazel or aloe vera preparation is an effective natural remedy.

✳ Sun Protection
Clothing
Platypus

SUN PROTECTION CLOTHING
T-shirts, shorts, all-in-ones and bathing suits made from fabrics with in-built SPFs save you from constantly slathering your child's entire body with sun cream, which can be tricky if she is wriggly and uncooperative (and many little ones are when it comes to this task).

You can probably make do with just one or two of these outfits for holidays as they dry rapidly. Look out for fabric that's breathable and if going for an all-in-one, something that's easy to put on and remove. These garments can be pricey but your child will live in them on beach holidays. Most stores will have some in stock in summer. Don't forget a decent wide-brimmed or legionnaire's-style hat, too.

UV SHELTERS

These tents are designed to block harmful UV rays on the beach or in the garden. We don't think they're worth buying because younger babies can be kept in the shade with a pram sunshade or beach umbrella and older ones are unlikely to want to stay in the shelter – especially with the lure of sand to play on. Moreover, studies have questioned whether some are as effective at blocking UV as they suggest, so err on the side of caution. If you do buy one, look for good ventilation to prevent overheating.

✳ **UV Shelter**
Shelta UV Sun Tent

✳ **Swiming Nappies**
Disposable: Huggies
Little Swimmers •
Reusable: Bambino Mio,
Kushies, Splashabout

SWIMMING

SWIMMING NAPPIES

If your holiday will involve dips in the pool, swimming nappies are essential. Unlike normal nappies, they don't swell up and weigh your baby down. Choose between disposable and washable versions. If you go for washables, you'll need to think about laundry arrangements if they do get soiled.

SWIMMING AIDS AND CLOTHING

There are now far better swimming aids than those uncomfortable-to-put-on arm bands most of us endured as children. Modern roll-on versions go on much easier without annoying the wearer's little arms. An alternative is a buoyancy jacket; these are rather more expensive but worth investing in if you'll go swimming regularly.

For younger babies, swim seats are cheap and effective although some little ones prefer to be carried in your arms at least initially.

❄ Neoprene baby wraps insulate a baby in water and can make the difference between your baby loving the water or hating it.

12

SHOPPING FOR YOUR OLDER BABY

From the announcement of your impending parenthood onwards, countless well-wishers have probably advised you to "Enjoy every minute – they grow up so fast". Like many clichés it's a true and indeed savvy one. Before you know it, that tiny, mewling infant is a walking, talking, tantrumming individual and yep, you guessed it, needs a whole new raft of products.

As a minimum, there'll be a stack of potty training stuff, a forward-facing car seat and a bigger bed. Thankfully these don't all need to be bought at once, so there's much less of a shopping frenzy than there was around the time of the birth.

SHOPPING LIST

- ✓ Potty or toilet-training seat
- ✓ Toilet training items – pants, wipes, disinfectant, waterproof sheet or pad, step stool
- ✓ Toddler or single bed plus bedding
- ? Bed guard/rail
- ? Back carrier
- ✓ Second stage car seat

POTTY TRAINING KIT

You'd think that after a couple of years of dealing with nappy contents, you'd be blasé about pee and poo; however, the prospect of potty training is fairly universally dreaded by parents. Our job isn't to advise on the timing, tricks and techniques involved – there is plenty of information elsewhere on that. But might we say that, in our experience, waiting until your toddler is 'ready' will make it much less of an ordeal. The right time to cast those nappies aside is a very individual thing, so don't worry about trying to compete with baby X who was 'dry' at 18 months.

Essentials:

❋ *A potty or toilet training seat* (or both). See below. If you have a large house or flat, buy more than one so there's always one nearby if your child needs to go in a hurry!

❋ *'Big kid' pants* Let your toddler choose a design she finds appealing so she 'buys into' the idea of wearing them. Purchasing a size larger makes them easier for your toddler to pull up and down. Some people like to use training pants for extra protection in the early stages. We favour re-usable ones over disposables, as the latter are too much like nappies and don't allow a child to feel wet.

❊ *Packs of wipes/cloths and disinfectant spray* These are essential for cleaning up accidents.

❊ *A waterproof sheet/pad* Place one under a child's 'un-nappied' bum in the early days of training to save the chair/sofa/car seat from a soaking. These don't have to be plasticky (see mattress protectors page 97); you even can use your old carrycot or crib mattress protector for this job. Once you tackle night-time training, a good idea is to, once again, get a flat, non-plastic mattress protector and use it on top of your child's fitted sheet to speed up middle-of-the-night bed changes.

❊ *A step stool* This makes for easier access to the sink for hand washing and for climbing onto the loo seat (it also makes your child feel more secure when on the loo if her feet can touch the ground).

Useful:

❊ *A travel potty or portable toilet seat adapter* might also be worthwhile. The Potette Plus is a portable fold away potty (with disposable liners) and toilet seat trainer in one and is a worthwhile purchase to see you through this phase.

POTTIES AND TRAINER SEATS
Do you really need them?

Initially, you will need either a potty or a toilet training seat (a smaller seat which sits on top of the main one, and makes the loo appropriately sized for a toddler's little bottom, making her feel secure and preventing her falling in the bowl!).

Most children start out on a potty because it's less daunting and you can leave one or more (if your home is large or on two floors) close to where your child is, in case she needs to go in a hurry. Then toddlers move to using the loo plus training seat once they're ready. In this scenario, you need the potty initially but could buy the trainer seat later on.

If you think your child can manage the loo with a training seat (and a step to help her climb up) straight away, you won't need a potty at all (and this scenario means no potty to clean out).

❊ **Potty**
BabyBjorn Potty Chair
(high backed, removable inner bowl for easy cleaning and splashguard at the front. It is bulky, however, so you might need a second, smaller potty when going out)

You can either buy a separate trainer seat (the padded ones with handles are good) or replace your main toilet seat with one that has both an adult-sized seat and a child-sized one (this also means there is always a child-sized seat available for visiting children even when yours no longer need it.

When do you need it?

It depends on when you begin potty training; most children are nappy-free in the daytime by age three although most parents start gentle training at two to two and a half years. Babies in washable nappies often train earlier as they are more aware of feeling 'wet'. It's worth sitting your baby on a potty occasionally from as young as 18 months to get her used to it, even if training in earnest starts later on.

Look for:
Essential:
* ❋ *Comfort* If the potty or seat isn't comfortable your little one isn't going to want to stay on it.
* ❋ *A splash-guard for boys* Potties and toilet trainer seats should have a raised front to help contain 'spraying'!

Useful:
* ❋ *Handles and padding on toilet trainer seats* These will help your toddler feel more secure and comfy.
* ❋ *A high back on a potty* This could make a reluctant toddler feel more secure and comfortable.

Don't bother with:
* ❋ *Gimmicks* Musical potties aren't usually necessary.

'BIG KID' BEDS AND BEDDING

At some stage, you'll need to free your little one from her cot bars and let her sleep in an open bed. If your child has a cot-bed, this will merely mean taking the sides off, so you can delay buying a full single bed until about age five or six. If, on the other hand, she has a standard cot, you'll probably need to

PRODUCT SHOWCASE

A clever idea from the makers of Grobag sleeping bags is the **Grobag Stay On Bedding Set**, sold in cot-bed or single bed sizes. Its clever design means the duvet cover securely attaches to the integral fitted bottom sheet using a zip on both sides. This makes it easy for a child to get into bed, but, once zipped up, she can't fall out (so there's no need to bother with bed rails). The pillowcase is also attached to the sheet, keeping it snugly in place. The designs are attractive and the fabric high quality. It is a bit of a nightmare to put on the bed compared to normal bedding but worth the effort for its advantages.

move her to a bed anytime between two and three years of age. The triggers for moving to a bed are usually when your child tries to climb out, risking injuring herself, she physically outgrows the cot or she is night-time potty trained.

Toddler beds are available, which are smaller and lower to the ground than standard singles but generally we favour going straight to a full-size single bed. Toddler bed frames are relatively cheap but once you add in a mattress and potentially smaller bedding, they aren't great value given you'll have to buy a single bed as well later on anyway. If you're worried about your toddler falling out of a higher bed, you can fit a bed rail to help prevent this. The only scenario where a toddler bed is a sensible buy is if space is too tight in the bedroom to allow for a proper single.

BEDDING

Toddlers don't actually need pillows and, indeed, many back-care experts would argue it is healthier to delay introducing one for as long as possible. When you do give your toddler a pillow, washable, synthetically stuffed versions will be better than standard feather-filled ones.

A duvet, meanwhile, will be lighter and more practical than blankets and sheets; go for a lower tog rating than you would for adults. 4 togs should suffice for toddlers and you can always add a blanket on top. Again, choose a duvet that's machine washable and get a spare in case of accidents or for when the main one is in the wash.

When choosing duvet covers, it's tempting to go with your toddler's current favourite 'kiddy character' but consider that you'll probably want the bedding to do for several years, whilst your little one's penchant for Postman Pat might last mere months. Plain bedding and a few 'character' accessories might be a wiser choice.

TODDLER CARRIERS/BACK PACKS

Whilst front carriers and slings can be wonderful for younger babies, they can strain your back and shoulders once your child gets heavier. Switching to a back carrier can allow you to continue enjoying the convenience of carrying your child long into her toddler years.

Types:

❊ *Conventional back carriers* Similar to framed rucksacks, with shoulder and waist straps, these enable junior to sit where the bag would go. They're normally suitable from around six months of age when a baby is sitting up and has stronger neck muscles. They're relatively straightforward to use especially if you select one that is freestanding on the ground, making it easier to load your child into and get onto your back. However, they are very bulky and won't pack into a hold-all for a holiday or day out.

❊ *Soft frameless carriers* Ones such as the Ergo and Manduca aren't quite so practical for all-day use but pack much smaller. Unless you're a regular walker, we recommend these over conventional models. They're fantastic for use around the shops instead of a buggy, or to give an occasional break to a toddler who mainly walks. But they can be tricky to use at first. Getting your child onto your back is a bit of a juggling act, so get someone else to help the first few times.

Look for:

Generally, many of the considerations in our baby slings and carriers chapter apply for back carriers, too, so before shopping, it might be worth re-reading them. Here are some key issues for back carriers.

✳ **Back Carrier**
All-day hiking trips: **The Macpac Bushbaby, Little Life** or **Kelty ranges** • *For briefer everyday or holiday use:* **The Ergo** or **Manduca** (both also can be used on the front for a younger baby)

PRODUCT SHOWCASE

If you only need to carry your toddler for very short periods, the **Hippychick Hipseat** can be easier on your body than using your arms, spreading weight onto your hips, and also allowing you to keep an arm free. It's easy to use, strapping around your waist like a large belt with a platform seat on which your little one perches upon your hip. A hip seat isn't a replacement for a buggy or back carrier, but can be helpful on occasions where perhaps a toddler gets too tired during a walk or to carry a younger child a short distance without the hassle of getting the buggy out of the car. It can be used from around six months of age to three years.

Note, though, that although better for your spine than normal carrying, it is not ideal if you have a bad back. In this case, it can be worth borrowing a friend's to see if you find it a comfortable way to carry your child. If you do want to get one, given use will probably only be occasional, it's worth trying to pick one up second-hand.

Essential:

✻ *Something that's easy to use and get your toddler into* As with front carriers, try and get a demo in the shop or look for one online. If you're buying a conventional backpack, choose one that can stand alone on the floor so you can put your toddler into it more easily.

✻ *A carrier that's lightweight* so as not to add to the overall weight you have to carry around.

✻ *Well-padded shoulder straps* These will prevent digging in.

✻ *Adjustable straps* These are especially important if more than one person will wear it.

Useful:

✻ *Leg stirrups* These provide somewhere for your little one's legs to go, aiding weight distribution for you and comfort for her.

✻ *A sun/rain canopy.*

✻ *A sleep hood* This ensures that if your child falls asleep in the carrier, her head will be supported rather than left to loll around.

✻ *Pockets* Useful for stowing other stuff so you needn't carry a bag, too.

* *Something that packs away small when not in use*
  Conventional back carriers will inevitably be somewhat
  bulky.

SECOND STAGE/GROUP 1 CAR SEATS

Most parents are eager to move their child into a forward-
facing car seat as early as possible, many switching as soon as
their child reaches the minimum weight for a Group 1 seat,
rather than when she has really outgrown the rear-facing one.
Why? Well, everyone thinks their baby will be happier facing
forward watching the world. And whilst generally this is true,
what those happy front-facing babies don't realise is that
they're actually much safer facing rearwards in the event of a
collision.

In fact, at the time of writing, whilst the merits of rear-
facing seats up to age four are still being debated, there's such
consensus among experts about keeping babies rear-facing for
longer that we expect a change in UK law in the next year or
two. We anticipate that this will mean parents have to keep
babies in a rear-facing seat up to 15 months of age.

In advance of this, we still thoroughly recommend you delay
the switch for as long as you can.

When to switch to a Group 1 seat:

* Don't do it because your baby's feet are pushed against the
  car's back seat.
* Wait until your baby has been sitting up for a minimum of
  three months, as this indicates she is better able physically
  to deal with the extra stresses of a collision in a front-facing
  seat.
* Wait until your baby is closer to, or ideally at, the maximum
  weight (13 kg) for her rear-facing seat than the minimum
  weight (9 kg) for a front facer.
* BUT do move her if her head is protruding over the top of
  the Group 0/0+ seat. If she outgrows the seat in height but
  has not reached the minimum weight for a group 1 seat,
  your only option will be to invest in a combination group
  0/1 seat (see page 183).

✳ **Non-ISOFIX**
Forward-facing Seat
With harness:
Bebe Confort Axiss (rotates making it easier to get your child in and out), **Maxi-Cosi Tobi** •
With impact shield: Kiddy **Infinity Pro** or **Energy**

Do you really need one?
Yes, it's the law if your baby/toddler will be travelling in a car.

TYPES OF GROUP 1 SEAT
Forward-facing with harness:
Your baby/toddler sits facing the front of the car, restrained by a harness.

Forward-facing with an impact shield:
The seat itself looks similar to a 'forward-facing with harness' model, but the harness is replaced with an 'impact cushion' or 'shield'. This fixes across your child's chest and is designed to absorb some of the impact in a collision.

Many such seats are 'combination Group 1/2/3' models (see page 183) for use up to age 12, as you simply remove the impact shield and use the adult seat belt with them instead at the end of the Group 1 phase. This saves you buying another seat when your child reaches age three or four. Most seats of this type do very well in independent crash testing compared to conventional forward-facing seats with harness. Be warned, though, that some children will not take to the cushion across their body, although others quite like using it as a little play table. It's worth trying your baby in one to see how she reacts initially.

Rear-facing:
In Scandinavian countries, 'rear-facing for longer' seats are the norm, letting children stay in the rear-facing position even after they have outgrown their Group 0+ seat. While safer in a front-on collision, not all of these seats offer good protection in a side-on collision, so we recommend checking crash safety test information from *Which* or NCAP before buying.

You may also feel that your toddler will be happier facing the front looking out (but a child who has only ever faced the rear won't know any different and a taller toddler will be able to see through the back window anyway) or that you want to be able to see her.

Another consideration is that these seats are bulky and take up more room than forward-facing models, which can be

problematic for small- and medium-sized cars, or if an adult passenger has long legs as the front passenger seat generally needs to be quite far forward to allow space for a rear-facing child seat behind. Many rear-facing models can be turned around to face forward on occasions when there's a passenger in the front but this is a hassle that you won't relish if it happens frequently. These seats also tend to be quite expensive.

Overall, we'd say do your homework on these – their benefits are not always clearcut. If you can keep your baby in her Group 0+ seat as long as possible (towards its upper weight limit, usually 13 kg), then that could be a good compromise.

Look for:
Really many of the same things as when you were buying that first infant car seat (see page 134).

❋ *The seat must fit your car and others in which it will be used regularly.*

❋ *Easy to remove, washable seat covers.*

❋ *A one-pull harness.*

❋ *Harness tension indicator* Available in some newer models, this shows whether the harness has been pulled sufficiently tight to be safe.

❋ *A recline option* Whilst an infant carrier will be in a semi-reclined position all the time, a Group 1 seat will be more upright. A recline option will make the seat more comfortable if your little one needs to nap in the car.

ISOFIX

When it comes to ISOFIX, the same pros and cons apply as before and obviously you need to have a car with the relevant fixings. Overall, an ISOFIX seat will be considerably more expensive and heavier but will be safer.

COMBINATION SEATS

You can buy a single 'combination car seat' to cover both the Group 1 and the later 2/3 phase (from nine months to when your child reaches age 12 or height 135 cm (whichever comes

❋ **ISOFIX Forward-facing Seat**
With harness:
Maxi-Cosi Priorifix

❋ **Britax Duo Plus** or Explora ISOFIX, Recaro Young Expert with ISOFIX base, Maxi-Cosi Pearl with Familyfix Base (the Young Expert and the Pearl use the same base as their respective infant car seats so one base works for both stages)

❋ **ISOFIX Forward-facing Seat**
With impact shield:
Any of Kiddy's impact shield seats

❋ **ISOFIX Rear-facing For Longer Seat**
BeSafe Izi Combi (ISOFIX installation can only be used in the rear-facing position; forward-facing option is achieved via a seat belt)

sooner), when she will be allowed to travel with an adult seatbelt). Such seats can be good value versus Group 1 only versions of a similar quality but some don't recline so well for naps and can be less supportive for the younger end of the age range, as they tend to be larger.

Those that only use the adult seatbelt to restrain a child during the Group 1 phase instead of a proper harness or an impact shield (see above) will not be as safe.

If a combination seat appeals – perhaps so the grandparents only need buy one seat for use to age 12 in their car – the Britax Evolva 123 is a solid choice or the Kiddy range (this uses an impact shield) and there are ISOFIX or non-ISOFIX options.

CAR SEATS BEYOND AGE THREE

Don't forget the law states your child should remain in a suitable car restraint until she is either 135 cm tall or reaches her 12th birthday. For this stage, high-back boosters offer much greater protection, especially in a side-on impact, than booster cushions.

INDEX

ACKNOWLEDGEMENTS

The authors would like to thank their 'parent panel' especially Niyati Keni, Tracey Harper, Carl Smith, Julia Nicholson, Catriona Hughes, Sarah WIld, Karen Hughes, Tanya Steenson, Derek Ross, Jennefer Khan, Sue Breeze, and Karol-ann Hewgill. Thanks also to breastfeeding expert Geraldine Miskin, and our car seat 'guru', Chris May.

Carroll & Brown would like to offer a special 'thank you' to Abi Hutchinson, press officer at Mothercare, for sending us product images used in this book – and many others. www.mothercare.com

And to BabyBjorn for supplying images and products for photography p39,110,166,169,175,176. www.babybjorn.com

Thank you also to Cheeky Rascals, www.cheekyrascals.co.uk, on-line distributor of baby and maternity wear products, for sending us the following images:
p34 Korbell nappy disposal system: p43 Jahgoo bath support: p122,142 Outlook sun shades: p123 Playgro educational toys: p123 BuggyBoard ride-on stroller boards: p124, 125,126,179 Manduca baby carriers: p149 KiddyGuard retractable safety gate: p171 HandySitt portable booster seat: p177 My Carry Potty leak-proof potty

Thank you to the following companies for supplying us with images of their products:
p40 Cuddledry baby towels
p51 Medela breast pump – medela.com
p71 Stokke TrippTrapp highchair – www.stokke.com
p80 Silver Cross carrycot – www.silvercross.co.uk
p81 Natures Sway Baby Hammocks & Slings Ltd (Stella Blog)
p91 The Gro Company baby sleep bags – www.gro.co.uk
p115 Mountain Buggy – www.mountainbuggy.com
p133,138 Phil&Teds – www.philandteds.com
p136 ISOFIX car seat base, p137,139,140 car seats, Dorel UK
p140 Out'n'About – www.outnabout.com
p145,148 BT digital baby monitor
p151,155 Geuther stair gates and playpens – www.geuther.co.uk
p164 Galt toys playnest - www.galttoys.com
p170 Prince Lionheart – www.princelionheart.com
p173 Splash About baby swimming aids – www.splashabout.com
p180 Bushbaby Child Carriers – www.bush-baby.com
p184 Britax car seat - www.britax.co.uk

SHOPPING WEBSITES TO BOOKMARK

* **Mothercare.com** and **Babiesrus.co.uk** Both offer well-priced own brand and big brand products.
* **ebay.co.uk** barely needs an introduction! A thriving baby gear section.
* **Amazon.co.uk** Venture out of the book section and there's a wide range of competitively-priced baby gear. Also handy for checking customer reviews before buying too.
* **Greenbaby.co.uk** Eco-friendly and natural baby products.
* **Babyconcierge.co.uk** for an idea of what's rated as well as more unusual products you won't find everywhere.
* **Kiddicare.com** Wide selection of brands at good prices.
* **Jojomamanbebe.co.uk** Mail order/online baby gear shopping – a mix of upmarket and practical items.
* **Johnlewis.com** A wide selection of high quality nursery products, including some own brand products. Renowned for their customer service.
* **Ikea.com** Basic, practical baby gear – some serious bargains.

INFORMATION SITES

* **Tamba.org.uk** Support and information for those expecting twins or more.
* **Madeformums.com** Online product reviews.
* **Nct.org.uk** Information on nearly new sales, local pre-natal classes and post-natal groups.
* **Which.co.uk** Subscription only service including up-to-date information on safety testing and product recalls.
* **Parentdish.co.uk** Parenting website with features and information covering all stages from pregnancy through to teenagers.

WHY TRUST THE PRODUCT CHOICES

Both authors have a wealth of knowledge when it comes to assessing items to buy for your baby.

Caroline Cosgrove hit upon the idea for Baby Concierge (the advice-led baby shopping service in London) when, during her first pregnancy 12 years ago, she was confronted with an overwhelming choice of products of which she had no previous experience. She longed for some independent advice and guidance but there was no such support available at the time. Shop staff were either lacking in knowledge or appeared to 'push' certain products. So she made it her mission to really get to grips with the pros and cons of the various alternatives, calling manufacturers to find out more detail about their products than their brochure disclosed and really investing time and effort into ensuring that the decisions she would make would be well informed.This was the beginning of Baby Concierge – a business advising parents to be on what products best suit their needs, lifestyle and tastes. Unlike conventional shops, Baby Concierge is not aligned to any selected products or a fixed stock range. *What to Buy for your Baby* is an extension of this philosophy.

Liat Hughes Joshi, a freelance journalist who specialises in writing about parenting and baby products, and is *Mother and Baby* magazine's product test expert, had the idea for *What to Buy for Your Baby* after using Baby Concierge, when she was pregnant with her own son. She suggested to Caroline that they team up to write a book as their hands-on experience of trying and testing hundreds of baby products made them best placed to guide others through the seemingly impenetrable jungle of baby equipment and clothing.

What to buy for your Baby, makes their hard-learned advice available to parents and parents-to-be and takes the confusion out of choosing key items – from pushchairs, to nursery furniture to highchairs, for example – from among the myriad available. It enables readers to read about the many types of equipment available, their advantages and disadvantages, and to make buying decisions according to their own lifestyles, budgets and other considerations.

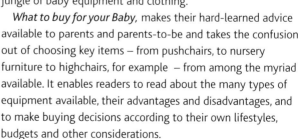

BABY GIFTS

You will, undoubtedly, receive many baby gifts, and in order for friends and relatives to be aware of the ones you need or like, we've included some detachable gift lists at the back of the book for you to hand out if you'd like. If you're not certain what to ask for, the following list should help. Remember to check the star buys in the book and add the requisite brand.

- Babygros/ sleepsuits
- Sleep aid (Ewan the Dream Sheep, Prince Lionheart Slumberbear)
- A large soft, apron baby towel
- Large muslin burp cloths
- Voucher for babysitting by a friend
- Sheepskin mat
- Sheepskin car seat/pushchair liner
- Pram blanket
- Large patterned swaddling wrap
- Selection of toys
- Organic toiletries for mum and baby
- Bouncer chair
- Baby gym
- Cot mobile
- Compact change mat pouch
- Bath toys
- Changing bag
- Sling/carrier
- Portable high chair/booster seat
- Nursery accessories e.g. wall stickers, pictures for the wall, lamp

Also available from Carroll & Brown to help you look after your new baby

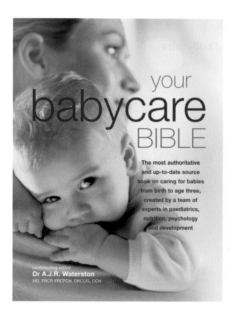

This highly illustrated practical guide enables parents to gain the skills and information they need to raise a healthy baby from the first days to early toddlerhood. As well as in-depth chapters covering all aspects of child-rearing – including feeding, cleaning and comforting – there are special fold-out pages, which demonstrate basic newborn care and first-aid procedures; a month-by-month guide detailing how your baby will develop over the course of the first three years; advice on promoting development, and vital information of keeping your child safe from danger and ill health.

ISBN: 978 1 904760 51 1

Available from bookshops and online at www.carrollandbrown.co.uk

CLOTHES

Sleepsuits
- ☐ 6 in newborn size
- ☐ 6 in the next size up

Short-sleeved bodysuits
- ☐ 6–8 in newborn size
- ☐ 6–8 in the next size up

Cardigans
- ☐ 2 in 0–3 months size (lightweight for summer, medium-weight for winter)

Socks
- ☐ 4 pairs

Hats
- ☐ 2

Mittens (winter babies only)
- ☐ 2 pairs

Scratch mitts
- ☐ 2 pairs

Bibs
- ☐ 2-3

Sleepgowns*
- ☐ 2–3

* indicates optional item

NAPPIES AND CHANGING ACCCESSORIES

Preferred brand(s)

Nappies

Cloth nappies (nappy inserts for two-pieces or all-in-ones/ all-in-twos)
- [ ] 18–20

Wraps (if using two-piece system)
- [ ] 4

Disposables
- [ ] 2 or 3 packs newborn size

Changing accessories

Towelling squares (to line changing mat)
- [ ] 6
- [ ] Cottonwool pads and/or wipes
- [ ] Lidded nappy bin or nappy disposal unit

Laundry net/waterproof laundry bag (if using washables)
- [ ] 2
- [ ] Nappy sacks (if using disposables)
- [ ] Nappy cream
- [ ] Changing bag or equivalent
- [ ] Changing mat

Baths and grooming gear

- [ ] Newborn bath support or baby bath with integral support
- [ ] Soft towel
- [ ] Baby nail clippers or scissors
- [ ] Flannel or sponge
- [ ] Baby bath stand (only if you have a bad back) *
- [ ] Bath thermometer *
- [ ] Baby hairbrush

* indicates optional item

FEEDING EQUIPMENT

Preferred brand(s)

Both breast- and bottlefeeding
☐ Feeding pillow*
Burp cloths/muslins
    ☐ at least 6, ideally 10 or 12
Bibs
    ☐ 3 or 4
Dummy *
    ☐ 1 or 2

Breastfeeding
☐ Breast pads
☐ Nipple cream
Breastfeeding bras
    ☐ 2 or 3

If you'll express and give breast milk in a bottle:
☐ Breast pump
☐ Breast milk storage containers/bags*
Feeding bottles
    ☐ 2
☐ Steriliser
☐ Bottle brush

Bottlefeeding exclusively
☐ Formula
☐ Formula dispenser
Feeding bottles
    ☐ 6
☐ Flask*
☐ Steriliser
☐ Bottle brush
☐ Insulated bottle holder*
☐ Dishwasher basket*
☐ Bottle drying rack*

* indicates optional item

BEDS AND BEDDING

Preferred brand(s)

First bed*
☐ Moses basket, crib, carrycot, or hammock
☐ Mattress
☐ Stand for Moses basket, carrycot

First bed bedding*
Pram/crib-sized flat sheets (not necessary if using
    sleep bags)
    ☐ 3–4
Pram/crib fitted sheets
    ☐ 3–4
Pram/ crib-sized mattress protectors
    ☐ 2
Pram-size blankets
    ☐ 4 (only 2 if using sleeping bags)

You will need the following from birth if you are
not buying a smaller first bed, otherwise these
items can be bought when your baby is around
three to four months.

Cot or cot-bed
☐ Cot or cot-bed
☐ Mattress

Cot or cot-bed bedding
Flat sheets (none needed if using sleep bags)
    ☐ 3–4
Fitted cot/cot bed sheets
    ☐ 3–4
Mattress protectors
    ☐ 2
Blankets
    ☐ 4 (only 1 if using sleep bags)

* indicates optional item

Preferred brand(s)

Newborn swaddles or sleep bags*
- ☐ 2–3
☐ Baby sheepskin*
☐ Cot bumpers*
☐ Cot separator (for twins only)*
Cat net (essential if you have a cat)*
- ☐ 2 (one for cot, the other for a pram)

OTHER NURSERY FURNITURE

☐ Storage (drawers, wardrobe or both)
☐ Changing unit*
☐ Feeding chair*
☐ Blackout curtains or blinds, or blackout
  cot canopy*
☐ New lighting*

PRAMS/PUSHCHAIRS
AND CARRIERS

☐ Pram/buggy with a lie-flat seat or carrycot
☐ Rain cover
☐ Footmuff*
☐ Sunshade and insect net (for
  summer/holidays)*
☐ Buggy weights*
☐ Sling/carrier*

* indicates optional item

CAR SEAT AND DRIVING EQUIPMENT

Preferred brand(s)

- ☐ Group 0+ infant carrier car seat
- ☐ Car seat base*
- ☐ Car seat footmuff*
- ☐ Sun blinds*
- ☐ Special mirror so you can see your baby in a rear-facing seat*

SAFETY ESSENTIALS

- ☐ Smoke and carbon monoxide detectors (if not already in place)
- ☐ Baby monitor*
- ☐ First aid and medicine kit
- ☐ Thermometer
- ☐ Medicine dispensing syringe or dummy*

TOYS

'Developmental' toys
- ☐ 2–3 (one that can be attached to the pushchair/ car seat; one hand held)
- ☐ Sleep aid*
- ☐ Bouncy chair*
- ☐ Baby swing*
- ☐ Baby gym *
- ☐ Cot mobile *

* indicates optional item

OLDER BABY NEEDS
(FROM SIX MONTHS)

Preferred brand(s)

Weaning equipment
Spoons and bowls
☐ 2–3
Weaning bibs
☐ 3–4
☐ Highchair
Training cups
☐ 2–3

If making your own baby food:
☐ Baby food blender or hand blender*
☐ Storage tubs and cubes*

Bathing
☐ Bath ring *

Toilet training items
☐ Potty or toilet training seat
Training pants*
☐ 5 (if using washables)
☐ Waterproof sheet or pad
☐ Step stool

'Big kid' bed and bedding
☐ Toddler or single bed plus bedding
☐ Bed guard/ rail or equivalent*

Transport
☐ Back carrier*
☐ Second stage/Group 1 or 123 car seat

Childproofing
☐ Items appropriate to your home

* indicates optional item

TRAVEL EQUIPMENT

Preferred brand(s)

- ☐ Travel cot*
- ☐ Portable highchair/ booster seat*
- ☐ Sun cream and insect protection
- ☐ UV protection clothes*
- ☐ Swimming nappies*
- ☐ Swimming aids*
- ☐ Protective bag for pushchair*

* indicates optional item

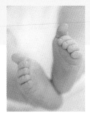

Baby Gift Wish List

Item   **Brand**

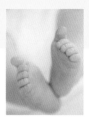

Baby Gift Wish List

Item   **Brand**

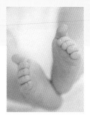

Baby Gift Wish List

Item   Brand

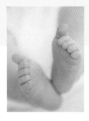

Baby Gift Wish List

Item   **Brand**

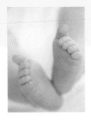

Baby Gift Wish List

Item   **Brand**

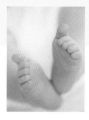

Baby Gift Wish List

Item   **Brand**

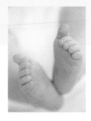

Baby Gift Wish List

Item   **Brand**

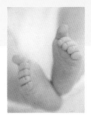

Baby Gift Wish List

Item   **Brand**